JEAN E. PATTON

with Jacqueline Cantey Brett

A FIRESIDE BOOK Published by Simon & Schuster New York London Toronto Sydney Tokyo Singapore

COLOR *to* COLOR

The Black Woman's Guide to
a Rainbow of Fashion & Beauty

FIRESIDE
Simon & Schuster Building
Rockefeller Center
1230 Avenue of the Americas
New York, New York 10020

FIRESIDE and colophon are registered trademarks
of Simon & Schuster Inc.

Designed by Hedgerow Design
Manufactured in the United States of America

10   9   8   7   6   5   4   3   2   1

Library of Congress Cataloging-in-Publication Data
Patton, Jean
  Color to color: the Black woman's guide to a
rainbow of fashion and beauty/Jean Patton with
Jacqueline Cantey Brett.
      p.   cm.
   1. Beauty, Personal.   2. Afro-American women—
Health and hygiene.   3. Color in clothing.   I. Title.
RA778.P295   1991
646.7'042—dc20   91-27159
                                                      CIP

ISBN 0-671-69386-7

"Harlem Sweeties" from *Shakespeare in Harlem* by Langston Hughes. Copyright 1942 by Alfred A. Knopf Inc. and
renewed 1970 by Arna Bontemps and George Houston Bass. Reprinted by permission of Alfred A. Knopf Inc.

In love and gratitude to

John Henry and Estelle Witherspoon Patton

whose unassuming grace and elegance glow

ever stronger through the veil of memory.

Brown sugar lassie,

Caramel treat,

Honey-gold baby,

Sweet enough to eat.

Peach-skinned girlie,

Coffee and cream

Chocolate darling

Out of a dream.

Walnut tinted

Cocoa brown,

Pomegranate-lipped

Pride of town.

Rich cream-colored

To plum-tinted black,

Feminine sweetness

In Harlem's no lack.

Glow of quince

To blush of the rose.

Persimmon bronze

To cinnamon toes.

Blackberry cordial,

Virginia Dare wine—

All those sweet colors

Flavor Harlem of mine!

Walnut or cocoa,

Let me repeat:

Caramel, brown sugar

A chocolate treat.

—*Langston Hughes,*
  "Harlem Sweeties"

ACKNOWLEDGMENTS

I am fortunate to have a pool of talented family and friends on whom I can call for love, support, encouragement, and hands-on work. I thank my cousin, James Richard Patton, for saying, "Yes, you can and I'll show you how," and for going to the library with me when I had only the seedling of an idea for this book and not a clue about how to get started. To my sisters Nartel Green, Olivia Patton Vincenti, Leslie and Cynthia Patton: your love, emotional, and material support have meant the world to me. Dominique Isbecque holds a special place as the person whose example inspired me to see color analysis as a worthy pursuit. Thank you for reviewing segments of this manuscript time and again. I thank Jacqui Cantey Brett for believing in this project, for being the writing companion and sounding board whose "Girl, you can't say that!" was always on time even while she was in the midst of another creative endeavor—the start of a beautiful family. Thank you, Clarese Peterson, for your high standards, high spirits, and great design sensitivities, for your work and motivation every step of the way. My life was easier because of you. I greatly appreciate the enthusiastic professional and personal support provided by my agent, Anne Edelstein. Special acknowledgment to Malaika Adero, my first editor at Simon & Schuster, for her belief in and commitment to this project and to Sydny Miner for bringing me through the last critical stages. For so ably organizing the stylists and models for the photo session and for reading (and rereading) and critiquing portions of this manuscript, Lisa Cunningham, God bless you. Thank you Lillian Caruana for giving me favorite pictures of myself—a rare accomplishment. Credit goes to our styling team of Dominique Isbecque, Jennifer Morris, Gloria Parker, Joan Phillips, and Raven Wilson who "shopped in our models' closets." For making their clothes and accessories work overtime thanks goes to Yumiko Okamoto who, as chief stylist, transformed these outfits with the special magic of her skill. Thank you Clifton Brett, photographer, and Anthony Jones and Marque Ealey, makeup and hair stylists, for that polished beauty you brought out in our models. Sherlee Argrette, Ethel Drayton Craig, Lenore Gall, Sylvia Grant, Angie Michael, Ed Noriega, and Joyce Michaelson Woods, your honest feedback and good wishes have meant much to me. A special thank you goes to Sherry Tolliver for finding the Langston Hughes poem and to beauty experts who shared their knowledge: Ty Greasham and Ross for makeup; Juanita Bassett and Marie Wright for hair; and Sandy Head for the "art of photo shoot management." The camaraderie and support of Carol Basa, Elaine Miller, and Pamela Pollock helped make the long road to the last draft easier to bear.

Finally, where would this project be without our "real people" models, who brought not only their beauty (and their clothes) to this project but also their patience and enthusiasm during the photo session. Thank you all.

Credits

My photo	*Lilliam Caruana*
Photography	*Clifton Brett*
Makeup and Hair	*Anthony Jones*
	Marque Ealey
Cyndee's Braids	*Juanita Bassett*
Arsha's red blouse,	*Kazu*
Cynthia's purple blouse	
Hand painted scarves on	*Chey Backuswalcot*
Cheryl, Patricia, Chey,	
Erica, Diane, Candy,	
Cynthia	

CONTENTS

INTRODUCTION

Women of African descent make their grand entrance into the world naturally decorated in a wondrous palette of rich and varied colors. The range and subtlety of tones in our skin is such that only a poet can capture their every nuance. We are color. Every woman of African descent should recognize the treasure of beauty in her coloring.

Color to Color will show you how to bring out the best in your complexion. It will guide you to the clothing, makeup, and hair colors that enhance your skin, your features, and your personality. Like many people, you may already have a good idea of some of the colors that look good on you or make you feel comfortable. But you may not know the full range of colors that bring out your beauty or why other colors bring out your worst features. Wearing your best colors will help you to:

- Project a positive and vital image
- Dress confidently for every occasion
- Explore new image possibilities
- Enjoy flattering attention and compliments
- Make the most of clothes you own
- Express yourself
- Reduce shopping anxiety and mistakes
- Overcome fear of color
- Be more adventurous with color in your home
- Save time and money

Color to Color brings these benefits and more to you, the woman of color. Clothes are your "second skin." They should reflect and project you at your best. There is no great mystery or secret to finding colors that will do this for you. The key to the mystery is knowing certain principles and characteristics of color and how they apply to you.

Why Some Colors Make You Look Great and Others Don't

Perhaps you've had an experience similar to this: You see your best friend in a wonderful new sweater. You rush out to buy one just like it. You put it on . . . and it doesn't work for you. You think, "This sweater is beautiful, what's wrong with me?" Nothing is wrong with you. It's just that while you and your friend may share the same taste in clothes, you may not have the same skin coloration. You both might appear to be medium brown, but when you look more closely you notice that her complexion actually has a reddish look while yours is golden brown. This look reveals your undertones and makes a great difference when it comes to selecting color. Your friend may look radiant in a bright blue version of the sweater but your coloring glows in bright apple green. In another case, you may have a relative or friend whose color seems different from yours—one of you is light, the other dark. But because you have the same undertone to your complexions you wear a lot of the same colors successfully. You will see from the models in this book and from looking closely at family and friends that a little more red or yellow or violet in the skin has a profound effect on which colors look good on them. The presence of these under-tones in a complexion is more powerful than the lightness or darkness of the skin—although that has a part to play as well. You will discover your skin tone's dominant color qualities in chapter three, "The Skin You're In," and chapter four, "Red—The Complexion Connection."

Color Analysis

Color analysis is a relatively new practice in the field of fashion and beauty. People who are trained to practice this specialty are called color consultants. They can analyze your skin tone and identify the colors which match, blend, and contrast with your natural coloring to give your skin a healthy glow, to brighten your eyes, and to reinforce or highlight your hair color. Well-trained consultants who understand color and image psychology can also provide guidance in the appropriate use of wardrobe colors for your life-style and career needs.

Color analysis became popular ten years ago with the publication of Carole Jackson's *Color Me Beautiful,* but the art has been practiced for over forty years, beginning with Suzanne Cayhill, internationally recognized as the founder of the "four seasons" approach to color analysis. But even her pioneering efforts were preceded by home economists who, as far back as the 1920s, were dedicated to helping people dress appropriately and shop cost-effectively by understanding the principles of color and design, clothing construction, and body proportion. It wasn't called color analysis in those days; it was simply considered a way to be a "smart shopper," to "know yourself," and to develop and refine the ability to appreciate beauty in everyday life.

Charleszine Wood Spears and Ella Mae Washington were home economists and African Americans who played a pioneering role in the study of how to select becoming and appropriate colors according to skin tone. Mrs. Spears was the head of the Home Economics Department of Livingstone College in Salisbury, North Carolina. Her book, *How to Wear Colors with Emphasis on Dark Skins,* was published in 1939 and went through five reprintings. Ella Mae Washington's book, *Color in Dress for Dark-Skinned People,* was published in 1949. It was based on her 1941 masters' dissertation. Mrs. Spears and Mrs. Washington were color experts who used their extensive understanding of the principles of art and design along with their own studies and observations of African American skin tones. Each had a different way of categorizing skin tones and a different approach to the factors that affect a color's ability to enhance a particular complexion. Mrs. Spears emphasized the effect of a color's lightness or darkness against the skin while Mrs. Washington emphasized the level of a color's brightness. Finding the works of these ladies was a particular blessing that validated, encouraged, and inspired me.

My Story

In 1984, the same year I started Second Skin Color & Cosmetics to serve private clients, I received rigorous training in color analysis from dedicated consultants and trainers, Patricia McKeon and the late Suzi Leach. Their system of color analysis was based on the philosophies of Suzanne Cayhill. This system recognized over twenty skin-hair-eye color types, mostly Caucasian. I learned to create customized color palettes of eighty or more swatches for each client from an inventory of over 1,200 different fabric swatches. Each swatch has to be carefully tuned to the color qualities of each and every person, as well as to the visual impact of their bone structure and personality—talk about attention to detail. My clients use their palettes as a guide to selecting clothes, makeup, and hair color. I liked using this system because it was one of the few systems not based on a theory that lumped black, brown, and yellow people into one category. This intense color-by-color process makes you go beyond theories into trying to see what is really in front of you. This training gave me eyes to see fine nuances in human coloration. Additional training in color theory at Parsons School of Design helped me to see color more expansively. But, as the saying goes, experience is still the best teacher. I had important lessons to learn that would take me beyond my early training.

As a native New Yorker, well used to riding public transportation, I'm continually exposed to an amazing range of skin tones of black, brown, and yellow people from all over the world. The similarities and differences *within* various groups—Africans, Caribbean and African Americans, Hispanics, Japanese, Chinese, East Indians, and Filipinos—is no less amazing than the similarities and differences *between* them. Consequently, New York is a visual training ground for me. I still remember the first "color shock" I experienced. I was riding the number 2 train when I noticed a velvety black-skinned young woman wearing a top in what the rules would say was the wrong color green. And to my surprise, she looked fabulous. I found myself sounding out a big Arsenio Hall *hmmmmmmmm.* I stared at the woman—which can be dangerous in New York—to figure out why it worked. This experience, and many more like it, challenged what I had been taught.

My training had not served the special needs and uniqueness of Blacks, Hispanics, and Asians. Many Black women have come away from color analysis sessions puzzled and dissatisfied because they knew they could wear many of the colors they were told to stay away from. Most current systems of color analysis do not do justice to the skin-tone subtleties of people of color. Even now, when most color analysis systems no longer place Blacks, Asians, and Hispanics in one category, there are rarely pictures showing the range of our skin tones nor are specific fashion and beauty strategies suggested for handling our unique color patterns, e.g., the low-contrast look of ebony skin with dark hair or the high-contrast look of ebony skin and white or gray hair.

Color to Color, like other books about color analysis, recognizes that the color qualities in and the contrast levels between your skin, hair, and eyes determine the characteristics of the colors that harmonize with you. Unlike other books and systems, this book is designed to take full advantage of the unique color opportunity in black and brown skins. You will have colors in your palette that are not generally found together. Other systems do not recognize people with skin tones that can effectively wear fuchsia and orange, olive and cobalt blue, black and chocolate brown— just the thing that many black and brown skins do so well. This book's approach also works for Caucasians, especially if they are considered "hard to categorize." It has been exciting to share these ideas with fashion and beauty professionals through the seminar company I founded in 1986 —Color Education Resources. Chapter three, "The Skin You're In," provides more information on these issues.

Afrocentric Color Analysis

Color analysis in all its various forms has a fine history of helping women and men to see and appreciate themselves more. It's about self-esteem and the joy found in the beauty of color as well as about practical money- and time-saving issues of wardrobe planning and shopping. For African Americans this exploration of self and color has maximum benefit when placed in the context of the particular issues that influence our individual and collective self-image. Beauty is not simply "in the eye of the beholder" nor is it "only skin deep." What a culture promotes and rewards as the good and the beautiful—and what it excludes—has a profound effect upon us. Awareness of the forces that attempt to influence you is important in developing a loving self-image, which is the foundation of a feeling of well-being and beauty from the inside out. You will also have an opportunity to explore ideas and concepts related to the color black, the tensions that still exist between some light- and dark-skinned Blacks, and Blacks-as-blondes—a subject that sparks passionate debates. Chapter one, called "Attitude"; chapter two, "You—by Design"; chapter seven, "Makeup Magic"; chapter eight, "Crowning Glory"; and chapter eleven, "Image Success," address these issues and more.

Color isn't just a beauty tool. It is a force of nature and a form of energy that can bring order, excitement, beauty, and comfort to our lives. Chapter nine, "Playing with Color," will give you techniques for coordinating color. Chapter twelve, "The Color of Meaning," and chapter thirteen, "Color Your World," were included to give you a glimpse of this larger world of color so that you can include it more thoughtfully and joyfully in your life.

1 ATTITUDE

ttitude. African Americans know a great deal about Attitude. We may even have invented it and we certainly know how to communicate it—whether it's with our hands on our hips, with the movement of our heads, or the thousand and one things we can say with our eyes! Feeling disrespected definitely leads to attitudinal questions like, "Who does she think she is?" or "Don't they know who I am?"

Clothes are great tools for expressing attitude. Some folks love to strike fashion attitudes with just the right angle of cap, drape of scarf, number of rings, bracelets, and chains, or designer labels. And doesn't it take a special kind of attitude to carry off those fantastically shaped, often skyward-soaring hats worn by our ladies to church and club luncheons? Beyond the fabulous and the funky, the repertoire of African American culture includes the "can't nobody going to turn us 'round" attitude of Rosa Parks, Dr. Martin Luther King, Jr., and Malcolm X and all the unsung heroes who followed them. The Black Power movement promoted serious attitude. The accomplishments of our against-the-odds entrepreneurs, from Madame C. J. Walker to Reginald Lewis, show our "eyes-on-the-prize" attitude. Attitude isn't just about bluff and fluff. It's about the powerful influence of mind over spirit and body. We will need our strength, creativity, and humor to wipe out the last vestiges of negative attitudes that keep us from seeing and nurturing the beauty in each other.

The Way We Were

Even before the American dawn of "Black Is Beautiful" in the 1960s, we *knew* we were beautiful and we taught our children that they were, too. The evidence is there in poetry and song, in old family picture albums, and in the history of strong, loving families. Even in an atmosphere of social invisibility and separation, our cotillions and beauty pageants flourished and our newspapers and magazines kept positive images before us. Many of us grew up with self-esteem in spite of America's (and even some of our own people's) antagonism toward typically African features.

We are not immune to the desire for the psychological and social rewards that come with being valued and admired in the mainstream, beyond the confines of our own communities. Not surprisingly, some of us are scarred from overt and covert messages that say we are not valued. Toni Morrison's *The Bluest Eye* is a moving and tragic story of what happens to a young dark-skinned girl made to feel ugly, inadequate, and insecure. She becomes obsessed with wanting to have what she considers a symbol of beauty—blue eyes. Her tragedy has been played out in many different forms.

For a long time in our history in America, those of us who came close to the white cultural concept of beauty—light skin, blue or green eyes, and straight or wavy hair—were considered more beautiful and more acceptable by the mainstream culture than our dark-skinned, African-featured brothers and sisters. We have absorbed these social attitudes to some degree. Even today, some light-skinned Blacks choose to overvalue their lightness, using skin color and hair texture as status symbols rather than as accidents of birth unrelated to qualities of mind and spirit. It's even worse when other Blacks favor and fawn over those who have light skin and "good" hair and treat them like trophies that give social status to whoever "captures" their attention, friendship, or love. Equally sad, of course, are those of us who reject and taunt our light-skinned brothers and sisters because we wrongly assume that their very appearance is an indication of a "better than thou" attitude. On both sides, this is prejudice at best and cultural genocide at worst. Either way, we can't afford to treat ourselves so badly.

Self-criticism is never easy or pleasant. A prime example of its difficulty was the negative response some people had to Spike Lee's movie, *School Daze,* because it deals straightforwardly and humorously with skin color bias in our culture. Some people felt that the issue was too sensitive for public attention. Ironically, though, not too long after the movie appeared an African American woman in Atlanta brought suit against her supervisor—another African American woman—for color discrimination.

Why look at such issues now, especially in a book about color and beauty? After all, we've had at least three Miss America titles. In 1990, both Miss America and Miss USA were Black. Women of African descent adorn the front covers of fashion magazines around the world and sashay down the runways of Europe's most prestigious fashion houses. The problem is, we don't own those magazines and runways. We don't set the mainstream cultural vision of who and what is "in" and who and what is "out." Our "look" is a commodity that can be out of fashion again tomorrow based on someone else's agenda. Can we ever afford to be out of fashion to ourselves? The way we feel about our racial characteristics helps to shape the value we place on ourselves, what we admire, and want to be like, as well as what we reject. They involve our deepest feelings about ourselves. Our attitudes not only affect our own self-esteem but the feeling of worth that we transmit to others. Where but in the eyes of each other is it more important to see and reflect beauty? I think it is important for us to see our Blackness as a rainbow; and no matter where we may be within that spectrum, to accept and identify with all our brothers and sisters—from the blackest to the whitest of us.

Black and Beautiful

Black is a color that does not equivocate. It's a stand-up-and-be-counted color. It has edges and depth. Black is the color that most clearly represents darkness and therefore evokes the fear and terror associated with it. As the perfect opposite of white's visual qualities, the negative side of black is further reinforced. Black's positive qualities of strength, power, and dignity are almost totally obscured except in the arena of fashion. But this is hardly a sufficient counterbalance. In fact, as late as 1988, studies done by psychologists Drs. Derek and Darlene Hopson found an extremely high percentage of Black preschoolers who could not or would not identify with this color. The negative associations are so pervasive that color psychologist Dr. Deborah Sharpe stated in her book, *The Psychology of Color and Design,* that using "Black" as a racial identifier was a disservice to our efforts at social acceptance. There is nothing inevitable about this. Black, featured boldly in so many flags of Africa, is a proud representation of skin color, mother country, and power. Africans seem not to internalize negative associations of black. In fact, for them black symbolizes maturity, fertility, and completeness. The smoothness and sheen of that beautiful dark skin are important symbols of beauty, health, and strength. Similarly, many Caucasians who complain about looking pale or "washed out" and in need of sun and cosmetics for beautification do not internalize the negative associations of white—sterility, coldness, and weakness. Nor do they project them onto their culture. Yet the negative associations of black hang around our lives and culture with the sticky tenacity of the tar from a Brer Rabbit story! We may not control the headlines that scream "Black Monday" but we can control our own speech, which sometimes links black with other negative concepts and expressions. Our children will learn from that as much as from anything else.

We also need to be aware that black has positive, powerful, and deeply spiritual associations. In ancient mystic thought Black is Divine Darkness. It is Alpha and Omega. It is the Most Holy Place before the Light of Creation and it is the place after death, beyond the veil of everyday knowing, accessible only through the highest levels of spiritual development. As Light is the release and expression of potential, Darkness is the source, the containment and embodiment of All. "Let there be Light" was to benefit earthly life forms. But where did God dwell before He created Light?

Black magic has simplistically been linked only to evil doings; its more essential meaning, however, is that black magic is powerful magic. The Black Madonnas of Europe are a case in point. Although they do not have African features, they are thought to be the fusion of the ancient Egyptian goddess Isis and the Virgin Mary. The shrines of these Black Madonnas are revered as especially sacred and holy and are renowned for exceptional healing powers. Lech Walesa, who rose from labor leader to first president of a free Poland, wears a picture of a Black Madonna on his lapel every day.

As for modern magic, geneticists researching human evolution have traced certain components of the DNA molecule that exists in *every* human being back to their source in one woman—an African woman. Black is the first color of woman and the first color of beauty.

On Your Own

No matter how exalted our collective history, in the end we each stand alone with our perceptions of ourselves. You choose the messages from the larger culture and from your own internal gremlins that give form to your reality. While Lena Horne and Dorothy Dandridge were the acceptable models of Black beauty in their time (Miss Lena still is today), Josephine Baker and Eartha Kitt took their "too ethnic," "exotic" looks to Europe and created glamorous images for themselves and for the world to enjoy. You can do the same, closer to home. It's as easy and as difficult as making the decision to accept and love yourself as you are and taking the time and energy to learn how to care for and beautify that self. This book can help you see who you are and appreciate what you see. Only you can take responsibility for loving what you have, not because it's perfect or meets some cultural ideal, but because it is yours! Attitude.

2 YOU—BY DESIGN

You as Design Object

You are design. Your body has a distinct composition of lines, angles, curves, colors, and textures. It has a harmony all its own. Notice the sweep of your brow, the curves of your lips and hips, the tilt of your eyes, the crinkle in your hair, and the line of your shoulder. Spirit and personality enliven and bring added dimension to the appearance of your outward form. You may have strong features softened by a gentle personality, or a tiny fragile-looking frame that houses a dynamo of energy. Forget about "ideals." You are who you are, so make friends with yourself. Lovingly take care of the design that is you. Learn to celebrate your uniqueness. It is easier to do this when you can see through the sometimes funny, sometimes sad "conspiracies" that keep you thinking you should be something other than what you are.

Beauty—A Mad Fairy Tale

The naked, unchanged human form seems to be an affront to every civilization. There is a universal desire to enhance, refine, and adorn the natural. We do it even when our efforts to attain beauty require great expenditures of time, money, and even physical pain.

In the old days in Malaysia, teeth were filed to points, while folks in other parts of the world preferred them flat, laced with gold inlays, or knocked out altogether. Neck-stretching rings, enormous lip- and ear-stretching plugs have been used by various tribes in Africa. At one time upper-class Chinese women had their feet tightly bound so they would be about four inches long and would resemble a lotus flower. The "ladylike" fainting described ad nauseam in nineteenth-century European and American literature was the result of incapacitating whale-bone corsets. Some women went so far as to have a rib removed to attain the fashionable "wasp waist" of their day. It could make you grateful for just a few corns on your feet!

Another aspect of the game of fashion is an interesting concept called "shifting erogenous zones." At one time a full-sized figure was a highly desired sign of wealth and well-being for men, women, and children. However, in the 1920s, boyish figures became fashionable for women. Thin was in and breasts were out. Breasts came back big in the 1950s, but took a back seat to legs in the sixties. Legs disappeared in the seventies, came back in the eighties, and are still hanging around. However, breasts are making somewhat of a reappearance with the popularity of what arbiters of fashion are calling models with fuller figures—size sixes with "boobs."

Today, health and vitality along with youth and beauty are mixed into the idealized images. Rather than reliance on corsets and cosmetics, diet, vitamins, exercise, and cosmetic surgery are used to accomplish the new range of "beauty ideals" which are now presented as options rather than do-or-die commands. No matter how liberal today's standards, they still aren't broad enough for us all. The one thing of which you can be fairly certain, no matter what your color, shape, or condition—your best body parts will be out of fashion for most of your natural life! Few of us can be like Tina Turner, with hot legs in the sixties that made a serious comeback in the eighties and still look fabulous striding toward the year 2000!

Two factors stand between you and those who make money selling you on how to look like someone else: a strong and loving sense of self and the knowledge of how to make that self the best it can be according to *your values.* For some of us that stops with soap, water, lipstick, and a smile. For others it's a joyful embrace of "every trick in the book."

The Consultant in You

You are the expert on what you like. Your responses—favorable and unfavorable—to color, fabric, and pattern are an important resource that you can call upon to create an authentic image for yourself. There are colors that make you feel good every time you see them, just as there are those that repel you. School uniform colors are prime "I hate that color and never want to see it again!" candidates. Perhaps you've spent days or even months selecting just the right color for wallpaper, paint, and slip-covers because you are looking for a certain feeling or image. The last time you held a blouse or dress next to your skin and reacted with "No way!" or "Fabulous!" you were being your own color consultant. In all these experiences, you were responding with your mind, body, and personal color history. You were tapping into the natural color consultant in you.

Most people know a few colors that look great on them and some they should absolutely avoid. Typically, however, out of habit, convenience, or uncertainty they have lots of indifferent "I don't look bad but I don't look great either" and "I'm not sure" colors stuffed in their closets. In your quest to discover what colors and styles you need for looking your best, internal and external factors can obscure your vision of what is right and possible for you. Be sensitive to how habit, fashion, family, and role models affect you.

◆ OLD HABITS One of the amusing aspects of youth is its flexibility and willingness to explore and experiment with its image, changing its looks over and over again, often inspiring mainstream designers and style trends with its inventions. Contrast this approach with that of many adults who settle into a few colors and styles that work well enough because they are comfortable and familiar. Often it takes the dynamite of a significant life event to propel change: looking for work after being out of the job market for years, divorce, the aftermath of a new baby, a major promotion, starting a new career or business, or hitting the "it's my turn" time of life. You don't have to wait for a major buying spree to "lively up yourself." Small steps work wonders. You can introduce new color in accessories or inexpensive items like T-shirts.

◆ FASHION PASSION You see it every day, the woman in the latest hot color and style. The fact that the color is too drab or too bright for her or that the shape is not flattering to her figure seems like a secondary issue for someone who is focused on being seen in the latest thing. Is fashion friend or foe? Too often the answer seems to depend on the largeness of our pocketbooks and the smallness of our hips. Actually, it requires wise selection and patience.

If you have a passion for fashion, you don't have to give it up entirely. After all, the fashion world captures our attention with exciting ideas that we would never think up on our own. Just exercise judgment to see that fashion serves you. See that your best colors are near your face and buy your most expensive items in your best colors.

◆ FAMILY FOIBLES Our families have a profound effect on all aspects of our lives. Family messages from the past influence us in many areas of life—including the way we think about and respond to color. As children, the ideas and values learned (consciously or unconsciously) from teachers and the church were also essential to the attitudes we formed about color. Do any of these statements sound familiar?

- "You're too dark to wear that color."
- "People in our position can't wear 'loud' colors."
- "Don't wear that 'hussy' color while you're living in my house!"
- "Those colors are too dry and boring."

Perhaps you could create a list from your own experience. Listen to those inner voices to find out what you inherited. Evaluate those messages in relation to what is right for who you have become or what you want to become now. Decide whether they have stood the test of time. This book is a way to open up the world of color to work with your skin tone, your emotions, and your life-style.

◆ ROLE MODELS Admiration inspires imitation. People often study the stars of the music industry, sports, and Hollywood to borrow fashion, hair, and makeup styles—even attitudes—all to absorb a little celebrity magic for themselves. Closer to home, a desire to belong to or be identified as a member of a particular group can lead to adopting the group style and "color code," be it corporate navy, suburban beige, or Afrocentric red, black, and green. Be inspired, but be your own best original.

None of these influences are fatal to the development of a personal color and style sense. "Looking the part" or like a "member of the team" can help you function more effectively in business and social groups. Borrowing ideas from an admired personality and from the latest fashions indicates responsiveness to the current social, political, and design trends in the world around you. Adding these trends to your individuality demonstrates being in touch with yourself. It is your values and your design—coloring, features, body structure, and personality—which are the main ingredients in personal style. Let the ideas you borrow from others be seasoning and spice.

You—As Designer

As a parent, adult, or even teenager in our community, you help to build the foundation for our children's self-esteem. From you they learn about the personal qualities that make a person "good" or "bad," "attractive" or "ugly." Even the way we talk to our children about grooming sends them powerful messages. Rather than telling them to get the "ash" off their little legs, we can use a positive approach by telling them to bring up their pretty color (boys too!) by oiling their skin. We can use haircombing sessions to bond with our children and insure that they see naturally kinky hair as beautiful rather than having those moments be unpleasant or even torturous. Why not approach short, hard-to-grow hair with the same loving care as long, wavy, or straight hair? We should never give our children the impression that their (or anyone else's) skin color, hair texture, or features detract from how beautiful they are and can be, inside and out.

As designer, caretaker, and defender of our children's vision of themselves, teach them about our culture and history as you give them the skills to build a future. This will provide them with more power than any cosmetic trick or suit of clothes they could ever wear.

Personal Design Consultants

Color and image consultants apply the artistic principles of color harmony and design to the human form. They can broaden the base of colors that you can work with for clothing, makeup, and even interior design. They can also help you choose clothing styles that will balance your figure while honoring its natural energy flow. These consultants are especially useful for those who have a hard time judging color or the best styles and proportions of their clothes or who need an updated wardrobe quickly. Many style-confident people use consultants as a way to find clothes and accessories that aren't available in retail stores and to receive a level of informed personal service rarely experienced today. Consultants offer a wide range of services: color analysis, makeup lessons, personal shopping, figure analysis, wardrobe planning, and closet clearing. Some *color* consultants only do color analysis while others provide some or all of the services listed above. There are *image* consultants who include color analysis in their services and others who don't. Quality professional services can be costly, but they will save you years of searching and spending ineffectively. As in any other profession, some practitioners are better than others. Interview several, seek referrals, and choose those who show a respect for and understanding of your design—inside and out.

3 THE SKIN YOU'RE IN

 our skin is like an intricate and finely woven fabric—a blend of similar and sometimes contrasting hues which changes from one part of your body to another. Your skin—your body's largest organ—is highly sensitive to your physical and emotional health. It flushes with fever, passion, or embarrassment, pales with fear, yellows with jaundice, darkens with scars, and breaks out in red and purple splotches for any number of reasons! It also reflects good health, nutrition, and peace of mind. A flawless complexion has always been a major beauty asset.

The great variations found within humanity's coloring results from the mixture of hemoglobin (red)—an iron-based blood compound; carotene (yellow)—a red orange crystalline hydrocarbon also found in yellow fruits and vegetables; and melanin (brown)—a pigment cell also found in plants and animals. Red, yellow, and brown could be considered "skin tone primaries." All racial groups have the identical skin tone primaries. Differences in the amount and proportions of these tones account for skin tone variations. Albinos, because they lack melanin, are the exception. The permanent display of melanin in the skin and organs of Africa's descendants is an inherited genetic response to the brilliant sunlit conditions of our ancestral home. At conferences on melanin, African American doctors and scientists are investigating the possible effects of the abundance of melanin in our systems on behavior and performance. In people with lighter skin, melanin is brought to the skin's surface as a protective response to the damaging rays of the sun and is temporarily visible on the surface of the skin as a suntan.

The Language of Color

Like music, color has infinite variety. Just as the seven basic notes of the musical scale can be combined into harmonies in many different musical forms—blues, reggae, classical, country, rap—the three primary hues, red, blue, and yellow, combine with black and white to create millions of visual tones. Hue, value, intensity, and undertone are words that describe these tonal variations.

Most often people see and discuss color in very generalized terms. For some, the word blue includes sky blue, deep violet, navy, and even turquoise. When talking about skin color we may refer merely to "dark" or "light." Or if we're trying to be specific we might say someone is "red" or "yellow." However, you could line up ten "yellow" African Americans and find no two alike. To become more sensitive to and accurate in perceiving color, whether it's in your skin, clothes, a flower, or a work of art, the following section reviews the language of color.

◆ HUE Another word for color, e.g., a green-hued ink. It helps us know the color family of something: red, blue, etc. The rainbow colors—red, blue, yellow, green, violet, and orange—form the basic hue families. You can wear colors from every hue when they have been adjusted by value, intensity, and undertone to support your skin tone.

◆ VALUE How much *light* a color reflects. High-value colors reflect a lot of light, e.g., white and yellow. Low-value colors reflect little light, e.g., navy and black. Colors can be placed on a scale from white through shades of gray to black based on how much light they reflect. The value of a color can be altered by the addition of black and white. You can turn a medium-value color like "fire engine red" into "baby pink" by adding a lot of white. However, if you add enough black, that same red will be transformed into a deep burgundy.

Primary/Secondary (see color wheel)	Add White	Add Black
GREEN	GRASS GREEN	FOREST GREEN
PURPLE	LAVENDER	EGGPLANT
BLUE	SKY BLUE	MIDNIGHT BLUE

◆ INTENSITY There are a number of terms that attempt to capture this color quality, like *pure, saturated, bright,* and *clear.* If you look at the color wheel in the color insert, you can see that the primaries and secondaries (the rainbow colors) appear bright. They have no traces of white to lighten them, black to darken them, gray or brown to mute them. The opposite of intensity is *muted, cloudy, faded, muddied, grayed.* This quality is found in colors like drab olive green, powder blue, brick, and dusty rose. Besides having many steps between light and dark, colors can have many steps between brightness and dullness. Clear orange becomes a delightful sherbet tone with the addition of a very light gray and it becomes burnt orange with a little black.

◆ UNDERTONE This term describes the "temperature," the relative warmth or coolness, of a color. Colors that mimic the sun and fire—red, orange, and yellow—are considered *warm* while colors that resemble the water and sky—purple, blue, and green—are considered *cool.* Warmth and coolness are relative terms. Color can be hot, warm, tepid, cool, or cold. For example, red violet is a little warmer than blue violet, but not nearly as warm as orange. Even yellow, usually thought of as a warm color, has degrees. Marigold (a reddish yellow) is warmer than lemon (a greenish yellow). The point where warm begins and cool ends isn't always clear. Colors like blue green and red violet clearly have their roots in both worlds. Some colors like spectrum red (true red) are cool but not extremely so.

Skin Tone and Color Terminology

The color qualities described above have a role to play in understanding and selecting the colors that enhance your complexion.

◆ VALUE The skin tones found among people of African ancestry form an incredibly broad and beautiful spectrum from gorgeous velvety blue black to rich mahogany, from milk chocolate brown to lovely light pink, and from amber browns to delicate cream and ivory tones. How dark or light your skin, hair, and eyes are, and the degree of contrast between them, determines the value range of colors that harmonize with you. Have you noticed that when a color gets dark beyond a certain point it starts to weigh you down or harden you? Or that you look drained if it's too light? No one looks good in only light or only dark colors. Each person will have a range. Some can effectively wear a wide range of colors from light to dark. Others might do well in light to medium dark or medium light to dark colors. People with high light-dark contrasts between their skin, hair, and eyes wear a wide light to dark range of tones while those with low contrasts usually look better in medium, light to medium, or medium to dark range of tones. The color palettes for each skin tone group make use of this principle.

◆ INTENSITY Some complexions are like cotton velvet: they have a muted light-absorbing quality, and may appear powdery, dull, or even a little gray. Dry skins often have this quality. Other complexions are like satin; they have a jewel-bright clarity (*not* oiliness) that reflects light. As a general rule of thumb, those with bright complexions or high-contrast coloring can wear more intense colors than those with soft, muted complexions or low-contrast coloring. For these folks truly bright colors are best as accents. Intensity is a visually and emotionally powerful aspect of color. You want to use it wisely to project energy and aliveness, but not so much that your colors outshine you!

◆ UNDERTONE Some skin tones are very warm: golden yellow, red orange; others are more moderately warm: yellow; then there are the very cool ones: violet, plum; and the moderately cool: red. Just as there are colors that are balanced or show affiliation to both warm and cool, there are complexions that appear neutral or don't have an obvious undertone: pure black, milk and mocha chocolate browns. Some copper browns have a cool red–warm orange blend that responds to a wide range of colors. The warm-cool balance found in so many black and brown complexions requires a color analysis system in which there is less emphasis on either/or color relationships and a greater emphasis on finding the warm to cool *range* of colors that harmonize with a person.

The Fast Track to Your Palette

If you show a consistent pattern between your skin, hair, and eyes, you may find your palette quickly; go directly to chapter five to find out more about each palette. The "Personal Coloring Guide" below is designed to help you find the palette related to your color qualities. First, find the skin tone that seems most like yours. Langston Hughes's praise poem to the beauty of our many colors inspired the use of sensual, mouthwatering, fragrant, and colorful terms to describe our complexions.

To find the group that comes closest to your natural coloring, read the charts Chinese-menu style, selecting an appropriate description from the skin-tone column, one from the hair color column, and one from the eye color column. For example, you may select rose brown as closest to your skin color, medium to dark brown for your hair color, and medium brown for your eye color. That puts you in the Nile palette. It is not unusual to find that your skin, hair, and eye colors are not all in the same family. In that case, do the exercise again using only your skin tone or your skin tone and natural hair color.

Don't worry if you don't fit a consistent pattern. Many people don't. The Right Red Discovery Exercise in the next chapter will help you find your pattern.

◆ PERSONAL COLORING GUIDE

If your personal coloring is reflected in this group, your palette is NILE:

Skin	Hair	Eyes
ROSE CREAM/WHITE CHOCOLATE	LIGHT TO MEDIUM COOL BROWN	LIGHT TO DARK BROWN
PINK/ROSE BEIGE	MEDIUM TO DARK BROWN	BLUE
COCOA/ROSE BROWN	LIGHT TO DARK GRAY	BLUE GRAY
LIGHT SMOKY OLIVE		HAZEL

If your personal coloring is reflected in this group, your palette is BLUES:

Skin	Hair	Eyes
EBONY	BLACK	BLACK
VANILLA BEAN	DARK BROWN	DARK BROWN
BLACKBERRY/PLUM	LIGHT TO DARK GRAY	
DARK CHOCOLATE		

If your personal coloring is reflected in this group, your palette is SAHARA:

Skin	Hair	Eyes
IVORY	LIGHT TO DARK BROWN	LIGHT TO DARK BROWN
LIGHT HONEY	LIGHT TO MEDIUM RED	GREEN/BLUE GREEN
WARM BEIGE	LIGHT TO DARK BLOND	HAZEL
MORE PEACHES THAN CREAM	LIGHT TO DARK GRAY	BLUE

If your personal coloring is reflected in this group, your palette is SPICE:

Skin	Hair	Eyes
LIGHT TO DARK HONEY	BLACK	BLACK
COPPER	MEDIUM TO DARK BROWN	MEDIUM TO DARK BROWN
CARAMEL	MEDIUM TO DARK OR BRIGHT RED	GREEN
CINNAMON	LIGHT TO DARK GRAY	

If your personal coloring is reflected in this group, your palette is JAZZ:

Skin	Hair	Eyes
WHITE/MILK CHOCOLATE	BLACK	BLACK
ROSE CREAM/CHAMPAGNE	MEDIUM TO DARK BROWN	MEDIUM TO DARK BROWN
OLIVE	LIGHT TO DARK GRAY	BLUE GRAY
COOL TOPAZ BROWN		
MAHOGANY/COFFEE BEAN		

If your personal coloring is reflected in this group, your palette is CALYPSO:

Skin	Hair	Eyes
OLIVE IVORY	BLACK	BLACK
SMOKY PEACH		MEDIUM TO DARK BROWN
DARK OLIVE/OLIVE BROWN	MEDIUM TO DARK BROWN	GREEN
BRONZE/DARK COPPER BROWN	DARK RED/RED BROWN	
DARK HONEY BROWN	LIGHT TO DARK GRAY	

4 RED—THE COMPLEXION CONNECTION

nergy, sex, courage, birth, death, war, and passion. Such are the images and emotions that surround red. This color is a rainbow within itself, each shade bringing another nuance of feeling. Red is both a skin tone primary and a pigment primary used in the dyes for cosmetics: foundations, lipstick, blush, and eye shadow. It is an important link between cosmetic colors and complexion tones. The right cosmetic reds for you are the same as or are compatible with the red tones in your skin. How will you know? You'll see it in your skin's response. The right reds will appear to radiate from within and give your complexion a healthy, natural glow. The wrong reds will seem to sit on top of the skin, appear unnatural, and look as if you've put on too much.

Color Effects: The Bad

One of the ways you can identify your Right Reds is to know how the wrong colors can affect your looks. Wrong colors are colors that are in the wrong undertone or are too bright, light, dull, or dark for your coloring. The following is a list of negative color effects that the wrong red, or *any* wrong color, brings out.

- **Connect-the-Spots:** skin tone irregularities like blotchiness, blemishes, dark circles under your eyes, or a mustache over your lips suddenly appear.
- **Blow-outs:** your jawline and cheekbones look fuller and less defined and firm.
- **Fade-outs:** your complexion appears grayish and dull.
- **Nobody's Home Tones:** you do a disappearing act. You look drained, tired, and lacking in energy.
- **Warden Colors:** you look harsh or hardened.

You don't have to see all of these effects occurring at once to determine that a color is wrong for you. For some people only two or three factors will be present. You may be more sensitive to how color feels—heavy, draining, or hardening. Others are more sensitive to a color's visual effect—dulling or increasing the blotchy appearance of complexions. If you have been blessed with an even-toned, blemish-free complexion, you may only detect an overall graying effect from an unflattering color. It's important to remember that there are no "bad colors," only colors that are unflattering to a particular person. One person's "bad" color is another's best choice!

Color Effects: The Good

Surrounding yourself with your best colors is like carrying around a personal lighting system designed to enhance you. Here are the positive effects that you can look forward to when wearing your best colors:

- **The Ah! Response:** like a breath of fresh air, these colors enliven your complexion and energize the way you look and feel.
- **Balancing Act:** uneven skin tones appear more connected and smoothed out. The best colors also keep your features looking well defined.
- **Impact Power:** the right level of intensity or depth gives you dramatic flair or confident authority.
- **Kid Glove Presence:** the quieter, i.e., lighter, less intense and neutral tones of your best colors help you project refinement, softness, and quiet confidence.

Using the Red Chart

The Red Chart in the color insert organizes reds in light to dark sequences in three color groups: warm orangey reds—peach, tangerine, pumpkin, tomato, and terra-cotta—form the lefthand column. A balanced group of reds (neither very warm nor very cool) with names like shrimp, coral, watermelon, and true red forms the center column. Cool reds—pink, rose, fuchsia, magenta, and burgundy—create the column on the right. Use these colors as a guideline for determining your Right Reds. Gather samples of lipsticks, articles of clothing, or other fabrics that match the reds in the chart. These items will be needed for the Right Red Discovery Exercise which follows. The goal of the Right Red Discovery Exercise is to determine the range of reds most flattering to your natural skin, hair, and eye color. While you may not be able to duplicate every single color you see on the chart, it is important to have at least a basic selection of warm, cool, and in-between reds as represented on the chart.

Some people will discover a very broad range of reds that are right for them, others will find a narrow range. What's more important is that you discover the ones that produce the positive effects on your complexion as described in the section above.

Here's what you need to get started:

- Natural daylight; northern light is best. Avoid bright golden sunlight. Alternatives: full spectrum fluorescent, or cool white light bulbs.
- Neutral white fabric to cover you from shoulder to shoulder and from neck to lap. Avoid bright blue white, grayish oyster white, and yellowy whites such as ecru or vanilla.
- A white shower cap or a turban (or the same fabric described above) to cover your hair if it's been colored.
- A mirror in which you can see your image from head to mid-chest and from shoulder to shoulder.
- The Red Chart and the color samples you've gathered on your own.
- Try to avoid prints. Multiple colors and bold patterns can be confusing.

The Right Red Discovery Exercise

Read the whole procedure first. The fill-in chart (page 41) will help you organize your results.

1. Remove all makeup.
2. Drape your upper body with the white cloth so no other color shows.
3. If you've colored your hair, cover it with the shower cap or turban.
4. Position your body so the light doesn't cast shadows on your face.
5. Avoid sitting or standing near a wall with a strong color that can reflect onto your face.
6. Place the color sample across your chest, close to your face. It's not necessary to put the item on if it's an article of clothing, this will simply slow you down. If you're using a small color sample, i.e., a fabric swatch, hold it in different positions around your face to see its effect on you.
7. Your goal is to determine which group of reds looks best on you *in comparison to the other reds.* Follow these steps:

    A. Technique I: Try to eliminate one group. Gather together several of the warm samples. Do the same with the cool ones. Compare the response of your skin to each group. Can you easily eliminate the warm or the cool group? Many of you will be able to do so. Run the Good Effects and Bad Effects checklists through your mind as you compare the results.

    B. Technique II: You can do a color-by-color comparison: lightest warm against the lightest cool, medium warm against medium cool. Compare the darkest shades last.

8. Once you have found your basic group, i.e., warm, cool, or intermediate, you must then decide whether all the shades in that group are equally flattering or whether you look best in the light to medium or medium to dark range. For example, if you tested best in the cool colors, your next decision is whether you look great in all of them or best in pink or the medium rose shade. Does the darkest one dull your complexion or give you the "warden" effect? Use the Right Red Discovery Form that follows to record your findings.

♦ RIGHT RED DISCOVERY FORM

Use the following rating system to indicate your assessment:

Best (B):	Your skin lights up
Good (G):	Pleasant effects
Borderline (BL):	Indifferent—but not very bad
Not Good (NG):	Negative effects are clearly visible

	Warm Reds	*Balanced Reds*	*Cool Reds*
LIGHT			
MEDIUM LIGHT			
MEDIUM			
MEDIUM DARK			
DARK			

There are several possible response patterns. You may find that you look wonderful in mostly warm or mostly cool. Some of you who have this kind of clear pattern of responses may also discover one or two good colors in the intermediate group as well. A few individuals will find that neither the extreme warm nor the extreme cool group feels quite right. These people are candidates for the center group of balanced colors. They too may, however, find they can branch out to a few colors in either the warm *or* cool colors. Finally, you may be one of those lucky people who, like Pansy, look good in many warm, cool, and balanced colors.

This is what the Right Red chart would look like for Chey, our Spice model featured in the color insert.

	Warm Reds	*Balanced Reds*	*Cool Reds*
LIGHT	NG	NG	NG
MEDIUM LIGHT	B	BL	NG
MEDIUM	B	G	NG
MEDIUM DARK	B	B	BL
DARK	G	——	NG

Note: This is a focused pattern—clearly warm colors are best, with a few of the deeper balanced reds as well. Light colors, even warm ones, do not bring out the strength and drama of this Spice lady.

This chart is for Pansy, the model for Calypso in the insert.

	Warm Reds	*Balanced Reds*	*Cool Reds*
LIGHT	BL	NG	NG
MEDIUM LIGHT	G	G	G
MEDIUM	G	B	B
MEDIUM DARK	B	B	BL
DARK	G	——	NG

Note: Can she wear color! Her everything-goes spread is fairly typical of the Calypso palette.

Hair Color Check

Once you have selected your reds, check them against your current hair color for compatibility. Take off your hair covering and put the color samples near your hair one by one. If warm reds are your best, then your hair color should have a warm cast and work harmoniously with those reds. If you look great in cool reds and have bright auburn hair or if warm colors are best and your hair tone is a cool burgundy red, you have some new decisions to make. If your current hair color looks unnatural and clashes with your best colors, use the Hair Color and Highlight Chart on page 87 to help you choose a new one.

Seeing Red About Red

Red is a wonderfully alive color that can be included in every wardrobe in major and minor ways. But what do you do if you're not really a "red person"? It depends. Red is often mentioned as a color that many people are afraid to wear. If you're simply not accustomed to wearing the color, relax and give it a chance. Sometimes it's a question of how we think. Red often conjures up images of fire-engine brightness. It is possible to forget that the more subdued tones like rose and burgundy are red, too. You don't have to take a giant step into the brightest red possible; you can start with a light or muted tone in your red family. When you're using cosmetics, you can always blot a lipstick to subdue it or apply a less-than-usual amount of blush and blend it very thoroughly. Of course, you can leave red completely out of your wardrobe, but you might consider trying the lightest pinks and peaches compatible with the depth of your skin color or the most understated and muted versions of your best reds, such as muted corals, brick reds, burnt orange, or subdued magenta. You might also try a not-too-shiny lip gloss that has just a hint of one of your reds or small amounts of red as an accent color, e.g., in your jewelry or as part of a print in an accessory item like a scarf.

From Red to the Rainbow

The "temperature" of your red is directly related to the temperature of the other colors that become you. The warmer the reds, the warmer the overall tone of the other colors that flatter you; if you look good in cool reds, your blues, greens, and yellows will also be cool. If you wear intermediate reds best, the palette that mixes the most warm and cool colors is for you. In the next chapter you will find colors organized into palettes of kindred hues, i.e., colors closely related by undertone, value, and intensity. These palettes are your key to coordinating a wardrobe that makes you look fabulous.

The chart below shows the relationship between your best red and your palette. There should be consistency from one group to the next.

◆ THE RED GUIDE TO YOUR PALETTE

If these are your reds	*Then this is your palette*
LIGHT TO MEDIUM WARM	SAHARA
MEDIUM TO DARK WARM	SPICE
LIGHT TO MEDIUM COOL	NILE
MEDIUM TO DARK COOL	BLUES
LIGHT TO DARK COOL	JAZZ
WARM AND COOL OR BALANCED	CALYPSO

Summary

- Your Right Reds will match or be compatible with the red tones in your skin.
- Colors that are right for you will appear to even out your skin tone and bring more liveliness to your complexion.
- Colors that don't flatter you emphasize complexion problems.

5 YOUR PALETTE— YOUR RAINBOW

he palette names are inspired by some aspect of African or Caribbean American culture: music—Jazz, Blues, Calypso; ancient ancestral places—the Sahara and the Nile; or a quality that is often in our cuisine (and our attitudes)—Spice. Each palette contains the same rainbow hues: red, orange, yellow, green, blue, and violet. But in each palette, the undertone, value, and intensity of these hues have been transformed so that they will harmonize with *you*.

Turn to the palettes in the color insert. Each palette has twenty-four colors—a group of reds, then light, medium, and neutral colors. They each have a distinctive tone or feeling created by their value, intensity, and undertone differences. You will find that the words used to describe the colors are often imprecise—medium light, somewhat muted, clear but not bright, warm but not hot—to capture the supple, often ambiguous aspects of color.

There are obvious differences between some color palettes and very delicate differences between others. Nile and Sahara are the lightest palettes, Blues is the darkest, and Jazz the brightest. Calypso has the broadest mix of warm and cool colors and Spice is the "hottest." Although each palette projects its own emotional quality, temperature, i.e., relative warmth and coolness, is an effective way of looking at palette differences:

Warm Dominant Palettes

SAHARA
   CLEAR AND LIVELY, BALANCING
   VITALITY AND REFINEMENT
SPICE
   VIBRANT YET BURNISHED, PROJECTING
   A FIERY QUALITY

Cool Dominant Palettes

NILE
   SOFT AND ELEGANT, BLENDING
   FEMININITY AND DEPTH
BLUES
   RICH, REGAL, AND DIGNIFIED
JAZZ
   DAZZLING, ELECTRIC, AND DRAMATIC

Warm and Cool Palette

CALYPSO
   SPIRITED, VIVID, ALIVE

For each palette there is a model whose skin, hair, and eye color is representative of people who belong in that palette. That same person also appears with one or more women who have different characteristics, but who also fit that palette. Because there are small but very real differences between people in the same palette, you must check each color's appropriateness for you. Turn to the color insert. In the Spice palette, for example, Chey wears all the orange tones well but in the Extended Spice Family, Esther looks best in the *red* orange shades. Candy, from the Sahara Extended Family, also wears some Spice colors. After you've read the information about your palette, read about the other ones, too. You will learn a lot by comparing their similarities and differences.

Tanning definitely alters your relationship to color. It can eliminate the surface yellow in your complexion and bring up red and orange undertones. Tanning can also make warm complexions appear more neutral. If you select your colors while you are tan, recheck them when your normal color has returned. Sheana, our Extended Calypso Family model, turns a toasty brown after some time in the sun and can wear more and brighter warm colors in her wardrobe, makeup, and even hair color.

Color-Style Strategy

Would you use the same type of frame for a picture of a Haitian market scene, a delicate watercolor, and a Japanese print? Not likely. You would choose frames that would support the color, the design, and the emotional feel of the pictures to show each of them off to maximum effect. Consider clothes your frame. For each palette there is a "Color-Style Strategy" section with suggestions for working with your physical qualities and personality. You want to set up a relationship between yourself and your clothes so that *you* are the star, not what you're wearing. People should remember that you looked smashing, not that you had on a smashing outfit. To achieve this, there needs to be a balance between the energy projected by what you wear—the brightness of the colors and the strength of style lines and details—and the energy of your personality and body. We've all been in situations where we see someone wearing a color that we notice before their features come into focus, or, a strong-featured woman decked out in frills and bows. Color strategies are suggested for "extremes," those with a forceful, dynamic, or dramatic presence or those with a quiet, retiring, or shy presence. These extremes provide a benchmark or perspective from which you can draw your own picture. The following attributes contribute to creating a dramatic, dynamic presence: a dynamic personality, a large or tall body, an angular body frame, large, angular, or chiseled facial features, very quick and sure movements. The attributes that create a gentle, shy, refined presence: a quiet or shy personality, a petite, slender, or willowy body frame, youthfulness, rounded and softly molded features, languid, slow, or hesitant movement.

Some people will find that they fit neatly into one category or another. But most of us are mixtures of strong and soft attributes. It's what makes us unique and interesting. All you have to do is notice when colors look too hard on you, creating "warden" effects, or too weak, giving you a "nobody's home" appearance.

Get Acquainted with Your Palette

Visually walk around in your palette. Never mind what it is called for the moment. What does it feel like to you? Does your palette remind you of something—a place, mood, a favorite piece of music, a poem, time of day, or season? Which colors do you like the most and the least? Do you know why? Which ones are you already using? Does your present wardrobe work with your palette colors? Place a garment next to or on top of your palette and you will see whether it clashes, reflects colors that are already there, feels bright or dull by comparison. In chapter ten, "Wardrobe Workout," you will find specific recommendations for integrating your palette colors with the current colors in your wardrobe. Are there any surprises? Sometimes people are really shocked to find colors they've been indifferent to look wonderful on them. You may have favorite colors that don't show up in your palette. Colors that lift your spirits should not be banished from your life. They can make excellent colors in accessories. Chapter nine, "Playing with Color," provides guidelines for coordinating color. These colors can also be used in your environment. Chapter thirteen, "Color Your World," shows you how.

Your Rainbow

I've also included a "rainbow" of additional colors to expand your vision of choices.

Every company in every industry from cosmetics to automotives creates color names to suit their needs, so it's hard to really know what a color is by its name. Southwest Sand in one company's promotional theme could be New England Beige in another's. However, as a general guide, I've used fairly typical color names, organized by hue family, to give you a feeling for your colors and how they compare and contrast with the other palette's rainbow colors.

Universals

Some complexions are truly difficult to classify because of unusual tones in the skin, an unusual skin-hair-eye color combination, or multiple tones in the skin that are difficult to resolve. If this is your situation, seek the services of a professionally trained color consultant, one with specific training and experience with the skin tones of women of color. Avoid systems that insist on either warm or cool categories. There are some basic color use guidelines that you can use now:

- Unless you are sure of a particular shade, avoid yellow; it's one of the most difficult colors to get right.
- Because you may have a limited color palette to work with, finding two or three neutrals that really work is important. Black can be very useful to you; use the guidelines for "blackaholics" in the next chapter. Also consider using lots of white in your wardrobe.
- Use low intensity colors; they reflect less color onto the skin. Use bright colors for accents only. Less intense colors will have a more subtle effect on the skin.
- Check you hair color; it can be used to emphasize or de-emphasize your natural coloring. Use the hair color guidelines in chapter eight.
- The following colors look good on most people of color: off-white, pinkish peach, pink coral, aqua-turquoise-peacock tones, pine green, soft purple (blue not red violet).
- Keep your makeup understated. Use neutral browns, grays, and blacks in eye shadows. Corals are usually flattering to most skin tones as is a very subdued matte red orange carefully blotted. Use those colors for blush and blend carefully. Avoid extreme color and shine.

Use your palette to bring new pleasure, organization, and order to your fashion and beauty life. It will help you dress with more confidence than ever before. Your color options will increase while you eliminate financially and emotionally draining shopping mistakes. Color confidence will help you explore new image possibilities, whatever your current age or life-style.

◆ NILE

Skin Tones
ROSE CREAM
WHITE CHOCOLATE

PINK BEIGE
SMOKY OLIVE
ROSE BROWN
COCOA BROWN

Best Reds

PINK
ROSE
LIGHT CRANBERRY

Best Metals

SILVER
LIGHT GOLD

Celebrity Model

ANNE–MARIE JOHNSON

The waters of the Blue Nile spray a perpetual cooling mist over the nearby hillside as it descends over the Tissiat Falls in the mountains of Ethiopia. This ancient river often evokes exotic movie images of Cleopatra's perfumed sails of seduction, but it is the cool image of water and mist that inspires this palette. The Nile palette is created with cool, blue-based colors that range from light to moderately dark and from slightly muted to clear. They provide you with energy and presence without overpowering you.

The first line in your color insert palette represents your family of reds: clear pink, rose, soft magenta, and raspberry. It also includes a cool peach, which along with the pale cool yellow are the warmest colors in this palette. Nile's colors are dominated by blues, red and blue violet, blue, and cool greens. Your neutrals range from light gray and taupe (cool grayed brown) to medium dark gray and purple. Navy is your darkest neutral. The best whites for you have a similar quality to your other colors —cool but not too bright: off-white, oyster, and antique white. Black in total outfits is too harsh for your coloring. The "blackaholics" section in the next chapter will show you how to use this color effectively.

Color-Style Strategy

Nile colors project a "kid gloves" feeling that goes along with classic, feminine, and romantic styles and images. This palette is wonderful for a rather narrow range of people who have a pink, rose, or milky gray cast over a light to medium brown complexion. This hazy quality in the complexion makes bright colors (usually so right with the high contrast look of light skin and dark hair) overbearing. The hair tends toward cool medium and dark brown or gray. Eyes are sometimes hazel, but usually range from medium to dark brown. Your particular constellation of skin, hair, and eye colors, personality, and life-style will dictate how you will use these colors. Like an artist, you can use your palette to create the image that suits you. You may find that you prefer the strength of the neutrals and the darker colors in the third column or feel most like yourself in the lighter colors.

Our model Cheryl wears the full range of her palette colors beautifully. The darker ones are excellent for the traditional business looks she needs, the lightest are especially good for blouses, playful casual clothes, or dressy and feminine outfits. The medium tones in the second column are the most versatile. When you combine color with the elements of style you greatly expand the ways you can achieve the look you want. For instance, Cheryl's light suit and medium-tone print scarf make her look very approachable and feminine. However, its conventional business design (straight lines, lapels, smooth fabric) worn with classic jewelry gives her look its professional polish and edge.

If you project a dramatic presence you may find the darker colors used alone or in combination with each other more to your liking. You can borrow from the second and third lines in the Blues palette too. When that is appropriate, use blouses and accessories in the lighter shades to soften your look. If you do opt for using a full outfit in light colors, give your natural drama some play with darker accessories. If you have a quiet presence, Nile colors match and reinforce these qualities. You can "power up" your look for work and play by choosing to work with darker and brighter colors in your palette, if not in total outfits (which can overpower you), then as accent or background colors in accessories, in skirts *or* jackets.

Our celebrity model Anne–Marie Johnson, a co-star on *The Heat of the Night,* is interesting because she balances many elements. She is really a hybrid between Nile and Jazz. Her angularity, height, and high-contrast coloring lean toward Jazz but the muted quality to her complexion and the ladylike delicate quality of character she portrays in many roles make a full wardrobe of bright, electric colors overbearing. She can use the deeper colors of Nile and the moderately bright colors of Jazz, avoiding the warm tones in the palette.

Accessories are important in building an interesting and versatile wardrobe. They can safely introduce contrasting colors and textures and playful elements into the wardrobe. However, when it comes to glasses, earrings, or anything near your face, use only your most flattering colors and metallic finishes. Glasses in one of your best colors, like blue or purple or even red, make a strong personal statement. Since Nile is a palette dominated by cool colors, most forms of silver are flattering for this palette's people. Because excessive brightness should be avoided, a large shiny silver earring will stand out too strongly, but when worn in a thin hoop it's graceful. Hammered silver, oxidized silver, pewter, and platinum are ways to get more subtle effects. Avoid dark and orange gold tones. Instead choose light gold tones. Wearing jewelry that mixes gold and silver is another option. Use the same concept in selecting metallic eyeglass frames, metallic evening wear, or even your car!

◆ THE NILE PALETTE RAINBOW

	Light	Medium	Dark	Neutrals *
Red	SHELL PINK	ROSE	LIGHT CRANBERRY	SMOKE
Orange	——	——	——	DOVE GRAY
Yellow	DAFFODIL	——	——	PECAN
Green	AQUA	CELADON	JADE	TAUPE
Blue	SKY BLUE	CORNFLOWER	LIGHT TRUE BLUE	NAVY
Violet	LAVENDER	PERIWINKLE	VIOLET	——

* Read the neutrals column from top down.

Summary

The Nile palette colors support you without drowning you out. Don't fight the softness. Embrace it. Work with it. Refinement, elegance, and grace flow easily from this palette. These qualities are never out of style.

◆ BLUES

Skin Tones

EBONY
BLACKBERRY
PLUM
DARK CHOCOLATE
VANILLA BEAN

Best Reds

ROSE
MAGENTA
BURGUNDY

Best Metals

SILVER

Celebrity Models

CICELY TYSON
MICHAEL JORDAN

The Blues palette is designed to show off rich dark skin to maximum advantage by using colors with enough depth and "sass" to provide these lush skin tones with the beautiful setting they deserve. Perhaps you grew up with well-meaning but misdirected advice to stay away from red and other exciting colors because you were "too dark" when, in fact, your skin thrives on color. The real issue for you is intensity or brightness: Very bright colors "bounce" off your skin and can create a garish appearance. The Blues palette has cool blue-based colors with just a few mellow warm greens and yellows included. There are a few medium light tones, but most range from medium to dark and the intensity level is uniformly clear, i.e., neither dull nor bright.

The reds of this palette (see color insert) are ruby and wine, magenta, and a very red orange. The second and third lines have deep blue, blue green, purples, and greens—including an olive green. There is a cool light yellow and a mellow, slightly red yellow. The neutrals are blackened versions of the other colors with the addition of a dark taupe, black, and gray. Your best shades of white should also be somewhat mellow: antique, off-white, champagne, pure but not bright blue white. Most members of this palette should avoid head-to-toe black worn alone. It's great as trim or as part of the main garment, as a background or accent color in accessories, or as part of a total outfit, i.e., as the skirt or the jacket. Always wear your best colors next to your face.

Color-Style Strategy

You can use your palette to create the image that suits your life-style, personality, and physical design. This is important because of the differences that exist between people in the same palette. Although the skin-tone range for this palette is fairly narrow, there are important differences. There are those with a neutral black skin with no apparent undertones, others with a blue or red violet cast to their skin, others who have a brown-black tone. Complexion texture differences also influence color intensity decisions. Blue's skin tones can be glossy, velvety, or ashen. Those with the brighter complexions can increase the intensity of their colors. Also, neutral black and brown black complexions can wear additional warm colors very successfully. Those with violet and blue in the skin should stay with the cool tones.

The overall tone of the Blues palette conveys strength, authority, and formal elegance. It includes the traditional power colors of the business world: dark blue, gray, black, and dark red. Elegance and chic looks are easy with these colors. If you have a dynamic presence you are well supported by the color tone of the Blues. You can also add bright touches from the Jazz palette and combine your colors for strong contrasts—like purple and black—to the degree that your complexion allows. The moderate brightness of this palette also makes it easy to project a softer, "kid gloves" appearance by using your medium and lighter colors alone and in combination with each other to avoid dramatic color contrasts. This strategy also works if you naturally project a gentle energy. When you use the "kid gloves" look as your basic style you can also borrow from the medium and dark Nile colors. Add the darker palette tones and Jazz colors to "power up" your look, if not in total outfits (which could overpower you), in a skirt *or* jacket, or as an accent or background color in your accessories. Our Blues Extended Family models Cyndee and Patricia are wearing light choices in the color insert. Cyndee looks at ease and elegant in neutrals: a light gray jacket over a black dress with a dramatically scaled black and white scarf as an accessory. Patricia's light pink blouse and delicate silver necklace form a dramatic contrast to her skin, beautifully showing off its depth of tone. Although it's a little sharp, its "I feel pretty" quality was hard to resist. Getting enjoyment from and feeling good in the clothes you wear is as important as getting the color right. Patricia also looks elegant and businesslike in the rich tones of her magenta suit with multitoned blouse in the same color family and black and crystal jewelry.

Glasses can be a fashion accessory; try them in one of your colors like dark blue or red. Since your palette is dominated by cool colors, metallic silver tones are wonderful for you. While a large shiny silver earring would stand out too strongly a thin hoop or some other delicate design would be effective. Hammered silver, oxidized silver, and pewter are ways to the more subtle effects. We have a long history with gold and it is hard to give up wearing it. However, some shades, especially the 22-karat and orange gold tones, don't blend well with dark, blue-based skin tones. Delicate gold tones or gold with a Florentine finish can work especially when there is brown in the skin. Jewelry that mixes light (14K) gold and

◆ THE BLUES PALETTE RAINBOW

	Light	*Medium*	*Dark*	*Neutrals**
Red	CARNATION	CRANBERRY	WINE	TAUPE
Orange	——	——	BURNT ORANGE	PEWTER
Yellow	DAFFODIL	GOLDENROD	——	——
Green	JADE	TEAL	EMERALD	FOREST
Blue	CORNFLOWER	PEACOCK	ROYAL BLUE	BLUEBERRY
Violet	ORCHID	IRIS	VIOLET	PLUM

* Read the neutrals column from top down.

silver or small amounts of light gold around stones in your best colors (rubies, sapphires, diamonds) all will work.

Summary

Do not let color outshine you. You can use color to show off *your* color by controlling the level of intensity. Your selection of fabrics can be especially helpful in this. Lustrous color will work on light-absorbing fabrics such as wool, cotton, rayon, brushed flannel, velvet, or wool crepe since they produce a soft sheen rather than bright shininess. Billy Holliday's way with the Blues combined sensuality with sophistication. What's your way?

◆ SAHARA

Skin Tones

IVORY
LIGHT HONEY
WARM BEIGE
MORE PEACHES THAN CREAM

Best Reds

PINK–PEACH
WARM ROSE
TOMATO

Best Metals

SILVER
LIGHT GOLD

Celebrity Model

VANESSA WILLIAMS

Once green and lush, now desert brown, the Sahara is full of contradictions: it is hot and cold, wet and dry, colorless and blazing with color. This Sahara-influenced palette isn't hot. It unites the colors of sand dunes and stone with cool blues and greens of Nile-fed oases. Its tone results from intense hues that have been gently bleached by the sun to serene shades. It is designed for warm complexions that need colors with moderately warm undertones. The colors range from light to medium dark and they are clean and clear to moderately bright. While suitable for a fairly narrow range of people, there are many different skin, hair, and eye combinations to be found within this group. The skin tone range is from very light to medium light. Hair color ranges from dark to light brown and includes a variety of red and natural blonde shades. Eye colors include light to dark brown, green, and blue.

The first line of your palette in the color insert shows your reds: shrimp, warm rose, tomato, and true red. Below that are lighter and darker versions of the same colors: blues, blue greens, blue violets, and yellow. Your neutrals include true navy, warm gray, a not too yellow olive, and several light to medium dark shades of brown. With all the possible skin-hair-eye variations possible, some people will respond to some colors better than others. Look at Donna of the Extended Sahara Family in the color insert. She has ivory skin that looks okay in the yellow and orange shades in this palette but looks best in the warm rose, tomato, and coral. Warm and neutral whites work well on this group: vanilla, ivory, but avoid blue whites and extremely yellow or browned whites like butter cream and ecru. Black can be hard on warm skins. Follow the guidelines for "black-aholics" in the next chapter to find out how to use this color effectively.

Color-Style Strategy

These natural colors have a vitality and youthful freshness that makes them feel especially right for casual clothes and sportswear; the navy, gray, olive, and true red fit nicely into the most traditional business settings. Fortunately, today's business clothes for women are more colorful than ever. This palette makes colorful business dress easy because it maintains presence without being too dramatic. In the color insert, Cay is a wonderful example of this in her cinnamon and blue outfit.

Your physical design, personality, and life-style dictate how you will use your palette colors. Like an artist, you can "paint" the picture you want with your choices. If you want to reinforce dynamic presence, you can use the darker and medium palette colors or you can soften your image by using your light colors in blouses and accessories. If you project a quiet presence, you may choose to build more of your wardrobe from the light and medium colors and save the darker ones for accessories. Increasing the depth and brightness of your colors and wearing stronger color contrasts will "power up" your look. But, do so carefully. You don't want to create harsh warden effects. Many women find that they tend to soften their colors as their hair turns gray. See "Cool Hair and Warm Palettes" on page 88.

In the Sahara Extended Family, Candy is an example of someone who can work between two palettes. She looks best in the medium and dark colors of this palette; she can even borrow medium-toned green, brown, and darker reds from the much warmer Spice palette. Turn to the color insert and notice how her hair color is emphasized by the red brown in her shirt. To bring more attention to her eyes she uses the medium and dark greens.

Our celebrity model, Vanessa Williams, illustrates how life-style and career demands can affect the way you use your palette. Her early Miss America pictures show her wearing a lovely blue gown that emphasized her eyes. The look was soft and classic and totally consistent with the look and feel of the Sahara palette. However, now that she is cultivating a career as a popular rock singer, she needs to cultivate a very different kind of presence and publicity shots show her in colors that are bolder, brighter, and darker.

Consider choosing glasses in one of your greens, purples, or even reds. Since Sahara is a palette dominated by warm colors, most forms of gold are right for you except those that are too orange. However, because the palette is mildly warm and does contain cool colors, silver tones also work well for this group. Check the amount of bright silver you can tolerate by trying different types. Hammered silver, oxidized silver, pewter, and platinum are ways to get more subtle effects. Jewelry that mixes gold and silver is another option.

◆ THE SAHARA PALETTE RAINBOW

	Light	*Medium*	*Dark*	*Neutrals**
Red	SHRIMP	CORAL	TRUE RED	OATMEAL
Orange	PEACH	TANGERINE	PUMPKIN	WARM GRAY
Yellow	DAFFODIL	BUTTERCUP	——	HONEY BROWN
Green	MINT	GRASS	OLIVE	CHOCOLATE
Blue	ROBIN'S EGG	TURQUOISE	TRUE BLUE	NAVY
Violet	——	PERIWINKLE	SOFT VIOLET	——

* Read the neutrals column from top down.

Summary

The Sahara palette is one of moderation. Its people avoid colors that are too bright or dull, too light or too dark, and too warm or too cool. These colors retain the strength of the earth and a lightness of spirit that allows great flexibility and individuality.

◆ SPICE

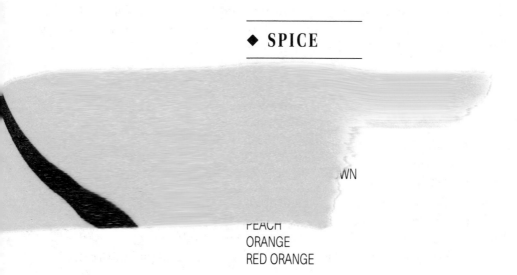

WN

PEACH
ORANGE
RED ORANGE

Best Metals
GOLD
COPPER
BRONZE

Celebrity Models
TINA TURNER
MALCOLM X

The earthy tones in the Spice palette are modeled after piquant, fragrant, and savory spices: saffron, ginger, cardamom, cayenne, cloves, nutmeg, pepper. They give an earth-browned quality to this palette, but it also has an autumn-ablaze vibrancy and a burnished quality. This is the hottest palette in the group. Spice was designed for those who need colors with a distinctly warm yellow orange or browned undertone. The colors range from medium light to dark and from slightly muted to bright. Shades of orange and warm reds occupy the first two lines of this palette in the color insert. There are no true pinks; spice "pinks" would be coral, salmon, and shrimp. There is an abundance of medium green, blue green, and yellows which have a little red, orange and brown in them. The only cool tones in this palette are a blue that has a little green in it and blue and red violet. Your neutrals are lush dark shades of green, blue green, and light to dark brown with varying degrees of red and yellow undertones. Ecru, butter cream, vanilla, off-white, and ivory are wonderful whites for you. Avoid crisp bright blue whites. Most members of this palette should avoid head-to-toe black. Follow the advice in the next chapter on "blackaholics" for guidelines on how to use this color effectively.

Color-Style Strategy

You can use your palette to create the image that suits your life-style, personality, and physical design. This is important because of the differences that exist between people in the same palette. The skin-tone range for this palette, for example, is fairly wide, from medium light to medium dark brown and freckles (orange and even gray brown) are quite common. Eye colors range from light to dark brown and take in many shades of green; hair varies from dark and medium brown to dark golden brown, and can include dark and bright reds. Flip to the color insert. If you're like Chey, the dramatic use of color sits naturally and easily on you. Or, you may prefer the burnished quality of Esther's colors in the Extended Spice Family. In our Extended Sahara Family, Candy's leaf-pattern shirt is a beautiful example for those who look wonderful in rich, muted colors. This strategy is especially great on those whose complexion has a matte quality that is easily overpowered by bright color.

If you have a dynamic presence you are well supported by the color tone of the Spice palette. In situations where you want to project a softer, more "kid gloves" appearance, use your medium and lighter colors alone and in combination with each other and avoid dramatic color contrasts. If you have a gentle image, the vibrant quality of these colors can help you project more energy. Use your darker and brighter palette tones to "power up" your look, not in total outfits (which could overpower you) but in a skirt *or* jacket, or as an accent or background color in your accessories. When you want to accentuate your natural quietness, stay with the lighter and more muted colors in your palette or borrow from Sahara's dark and neutral colors.

If you work in a traditional corporate setting in which the dark blue-based colors like navy, gray, and black are still the most accepted ones, use them as part of your wardrobe. It will help you to be seen as a member of the team. Use your red in a muted tomato shade and leave the orange tones for play. Adventurous colors such as burnt orange or dusky pumpkin may be fabulous in some creative business settings but, even then, they require first-rate fabric and design to be carried off with style at the executive level. Coordinate your beige, browns, and neutral (not too yellow) olive tones with black. Wear warm grays and find a shade of navy that works well for you (there is one). Use off-white and cream for your whites.

Glasses in one of your vivid colors would make quite a strong personal statement. Or select any of your neutrals: tortoise, for example, if you're conservative or leopard if you're not. As yours is a palette dominated by warm colors, most tones of gold are right for you. Bronze, copper, ivory, and wood also fit beautifully with this palette. Silver is too cool for most members of this palette. However, oxidized silver can work, as will jewelry that mixes gold and muted silver in the design.

◆ THE SPICE PALETTE RAINBOW

	Light	Medium	Dark	Neutrals*
Red	SALMON	POPPY	PAPRIKA	RUST BROWN
Orange	APRICOT	PERSIAN MELON	BURNT ORANGE	WHEAT
Yellow	SUNFLOWER	MARIGOLD	MUSTARD	DARK CHOCOLATE
Green	KIWI	EMERALD	FOREST	OLIVE
Blue	AQUA	TEAL	PEACOCK	TABASCO
Violet	——	VIOLET	PURPLE	——

* Read the neutrals column from top down.

Summary

Earth tones do not have to conjure up images of sturdy plaid furniture, early American farmhouses, or dull "nobody's home" browns. Think spicy and exotic: rich brocades, leather, suede, and ethnic designs from around the world.

◆ JAZZ

Skin Tones
CHAMPAGNE
WHITE CHOCOLATE
OLIVE
COOL TOPAZ BROWN
MILK CHOCOLATE
MAHOGANY
COFFEE BEAN

Best Reds
FUCHSIA
MAGENTA
BURGUNDY

Best Metals
SILVER
LIGHT GOLD

Celebrity Models
LENA HORNE
DIAHANN CARROLL
ARSENIO HALL

Jazz, even in improvisation, is sure, definite, inspired. Sharp or subtle, it is never wishy-washy, whether sung with the elegant sophistication of Sarah Vaughan or played with the brilliance of Coltrane. Equally definite, Jazz palette colors are pure pigment—strong, dark, and bright. This palette was designed for those who would be cheated in anything less than dazzling color. Cool red, blue, and purple colors dominate this palette, but warm green, yellow, and orange are included too. The colors range from light to dark. The intensity of the cool colors is clear to bright. The intensity of the warm colors is muted (browned rather than grayed) to clear.

On the first two lines of your color insert palette are beautiful reds including dark pink, magenta, red orange, and true red. Then come medium and dark shades of similar colors: green, blue and red violet, yellow and blue green. Your neutrals are light and dark gray, black, purple, dark blue and green. Your best shades of white are snow white, off-white, and champagne.

Color-Style Strategy

It is hard to create a "nobody's home" effect in Jazz colors. They demand attention. They easily support a look that is chic and dramatic. Black-and-white color schemes never seem to go out of style. This palette includes the traditional authority colors for business—black, dark blue, deep red, and gray. Worn in combination with one another, these colors make a striking high-contrast, high-powered look.

◆ THE JAZZ PALETTE RAINBOW

	Light	Medium	Dark	Neutrals*
Red	SHOCKING PINK	STRAWBERRY	CRANBERRY	BLACK WALNUT
Orange	———	PERSIAN MELON	BURNT ORANGE	CHARCOAL GRAY
Yellow	LEMON	SUNFLOWER	MARIGOLD	STEEL GRAY
Green	KIWI	EMERALD	PINE	BLACK OLIVE
Blue	CORNFLOWER	COBALT	ROYAL BLUE	MIDNIGHT BLUE
Violet	PERIWINKLE	IRIS	ROYAL PURPLE	EGGPLANT

* Read the neutrals column from top down.

A wide range of people fit into this palette—those with dark and medium complexions with dark eyes and hair and those with light and very light skin who have dark hair and eyes (or, occasionally, light eyes). Add gray hair to any of those skin-tone and eye-color combinations. With so many possible combinations, not everyone who fits in this palette wears all the colors with equal success or will want to create the same style and look from their palette. On the color insert page showcasing the Jazz Extended Family, our models Lenore and Nancy limit use of yellow from their palette. On the other hand, yellow would be wonderful on Erica. Your physical design, personality, and life-style dictate how you use your colors. Like an artist, you can use your colors to create the image that suits you. If you have a dramatic presence, the energy and excitement of this palette will reinforce you. When you want to create a softer, more "kid gloves" presence, use more medium and light colors from your palette, but anchor them with dark or bright accents. Don't let yourself fade. Also, use moderate contrasts such as charcoal and rose rather than black and bright red. This kind of strategy is often used by women when they start to get significant amounts of gray in their hair. You can "power up" your image by adding a darker blouse, jacket, or skirt, using a darker or brighter color as a background or accent color in scarves and other accessories—just don't overpower yourself.

Use glasses as an accent in colors like blue or purple or even red, if you want to be adventurous, or gray, pearl, or black if you're more conservative. Your palette is dominated by cool colors, so most forms of silver jewelry are right for you, from bright to matte finishes. Avoid dark and orange golds; choose light gold tones instead.

Summary

Enjoy the energy and drama this palette projects. Avoid any color that dulls or drains you. Yet even you, who can easily handle so much, must be sensitive to when a color or combination of colors begins to overpower your specific coloring or when brightness becomes harsh and glaring.

◆ CALYPSO

Skin Tones

IVORY-OLIVE
DARK OLIVE
SMOKY PEACH
BRONZE
OLIVE BROWN
DARK COPPER BROWN
DARK HONEY BROWN

Best Reds

MAGENTA
TRUE RED
TOMATO

Best Metals

SILVER
LIGHT GOLD
BRONZE
COPPER

Calypso has strong direct rhythms and sassy sly lyrics. It is cultivated in countries where nature seems to approve of her warm and cool colors dancing "back to belly": cool blue skies and hot yellow sun, lush greens, flowers, and birds of every description. Such places inspire the vivid colors in Caribbean art and the South Seas paintings of Gauguin in which the lovely shades of brown in the women's skin and the beautiful colors of nature form a seamless whole. The Calypso palette was designed for those whose color responsiveness is so great they would be cheated were they limited to an either-or choice between warm and cool colors. This palette has approximately a 40:40:20 ratio of warm:cool:intermediate colors. They range from medium light to dark and from slightly muted to bright.

In the color insert, this palette's reds include various shades of red orange, true red, magenta, and burgundy. Your second and third lines have colors that are a little lighter or darker like the blue and blue green tones. Or, they may be somewhat different versions of each other like the greens in which one is considerably warmer than the other and the blue and red violet tones. On the end is a balanced yellow over warm orange yellow. Your neutrals also reflect the dual quality of the palette: violet navy, balanced gray, black, a copper brown, and a warm and a neutral (not very yellow) olive green. The white shades that work for this palette are antique white, off-white, vanilla, and clean white (not harsh, bright blue white).

Color-Style Strategy

Calypso colors are dynamic. They integrate the warmth of harvest tones: brown, orange, green, and yellow, with the cool business colors: gray, dark blue, and cool red. This gives you great flexibility. You can easily enjoy unusual and interesting color combinations in addition to using the traditional approach of working with just the warm or the cool side of your palette. You can do all three. Pay special attention to "Playing with Color" and "Wardrobe Workout" in the later chapters of this book. They will help you take maximum advantage of your special color opportunity while avoiding the pitfalls of overabundance.

The skin tones of those who fit into this palette often seem suspended between two worlds: ivory and olive, olive and brown, and a mix of cool red and warm orange tones. Some skins seem neutral. These are not middle-of-the-road complexions. Some lean more to the warm side and others to the cool side. On the color insert page for the Calypso Extended Family, our model Sheana would add more colors from the Jazz palette. This is consistent with her high-contrast looks and slightly cool skin. When she is tan, the warmth in her skin comes up so strongly that she adds more Spice tones. Arsha, on the other hand, will add *most* of her colors from the Spice palette. Pansy's slightly red deep brown skin lets her wear the wide range of warm and cool colors. She borrows from the Spice and Jazz palettes, which have an intensity and value range that is close to Calypso's. The Nile and Sahara palettes are too light for her coloring and the Blues palette is too dark.

If you have a dynamic or dramatic presence, you can support that quality with this palette's strong and bright colors and bold warm and cool color combinations. For a "kid gloves" presence use light and medium colors from your palette, but anchor them with darker or brighter accents. Don't make yourself fade. If you have a soft presence, don't drown yourself in the brightest and boldest color combinations. Use more of the light and medium colors in your palette and less aggressive color combinations such as navy and beige rather than black and red.

Most members of this palette will wear a wide range of gold, silver, and copper. It will be important to figure out how shiny or matte finishes affect you in each of these metals. Choose glasses in one of your best colors, if you want to be adventurous, or from your neutrals, if you're more conservative.

◆ THE CALYPSO PALETTE RAINBOW

	Light	*Medium*	*Dark*	*Neutrals* *
Red	CORAL	STRAWBERRY	TRUE RED	IRISH LINEN
Orange	PINK-PEACH	PERSIAN MELON	——	CHARCOAL
Yellow	LEMON	SUNFLOWER	MARIGOLD	BLACK-BROWN
Green	KIWI	EMERALD	OLIVE	HUNTER
Blue	AQUA	PEACOCK	ULTRAMARINE	NAVY
Violet	LIGHT FUCHSIA	VIOLET	ROYAL PURPLE	BLUEBERRY

* Read the neutrals column from top down.

Summary

Learn to master your mixed blessing of warm and cool colors and you can dress with the appeal of a sunset, the inspiration of dawn, or the charm of a spring day.

6 PALETTE POWER

Enjoy your palette, but don't be limited by it. Use it as a path that offers a broad view of color. The human eye can discriminate millions of color variations. There may be thousands of shades that would flatter you. As you read on, you'll discover ways to personalize your palette, to expand it, and to make it work for business and pleasure, for your personality and your moods. Your palette can be a vital, growing part of your life rather than a narrow, limiting set of rules.

Color and Feeling

Colors singly and in combination with each other can create different moods. A few rules of thumb:

- Light colors project a soft, quiet, gentle feeling
- Darker colors project seriousness, weight, and depth
- Clear tones read as energetic, youthful, and friendly
- Bright colors excite and draw attention
- Muted ~~tones~~ suggest refinement, seriousness, sophistication,

~~colors~~ will suggest somberness or even depression

Naturally, the way colors are combined also projects feelings:

- Extreme light-dark contrasts evoke drama
- Light colors worn together are delicate, ethereal, sometimes vague
- Dark colors used together are sobering, heavy, and can produce a sense of solidity

A charcoal gray dress topped with a cool burgundy red blazer has a crisp business image. Change that red to a rich warm cantaloupe and the feeling is a little more mellow, approachable, and fashion oriented.

Not everyone needs or wants a power image for work. Teachers, counselors, psychologists, and others who work in one-to-one or small-group situations—often in small spaces and in close proximity to others—exert influence and leadership; the assertion of power may be out of place. They need to encourage open communication, inspire confidence, and exude a sense of competence, not to intimidate. What's the best way to soften up the hard power look?

- Use medium-toned colors rather than very dark ones; use moderately bright accents.
- Avoid high-contrast color combinations. Pair a medium gray suit with an off-white or light gray blouse. Want more color? Add a multicolored scarf or select a blouse in soft blue, violet, strawberry, or coral instead of the gray.

In a similar vein, if you are in the arts or a creative field where showing your talent through color and design is important to you, choose unusual color combinations, textures, and accessories. See chapter nine, "Playing with Color."

Be sensitive to the energy projected by your palette and your favorite colors. Learn how to use this energy as you decide what to wear each day.

Second Skin Colors

Your body is the source of your most unique-to-you fashion colors. *You can transform the literal color of your eyes, hair, and skin into wardrobe colors.* Leave the fireworks and power plays for other colors; these second skin shades have a lower energy. They project "kid gloves" feelings that are refined, quiet, and subtly sensual. Consider them a special addition to your palette.

Natural hazel, green, and blue eyes can be emphasized by repeating a darker or less vibrant version of their color in your clothes. Brighter shades will compete with your eyes and make them appear dull. However, intense versions of your eye color are effective in small amounts.

Natural brown, red, and blonde hair shades contain a variety of tones. Repeating them in your clothing is a wonderful way to select a neutral, especially in suede and leather. When worn somewhere near the face— but not as a blouse—hair-tone neutrals create a frame around your face. This strategy is equally effective for gray hair and hair that has been highlighted or colored brown or red. It is crucial to the effective use of this strategy that your hair color is absolutely right for your complexion. See chapter eight on hair color for guidance.

Your skin tone isn't a single flat color: it offers you a range of shades with subtle differences that may only emerge in response to the colors placed next to it. Repeating your actual skin colors works best for complexions—no matter how light or dark—that show some brown in them. This is not really a flattering strategy for those with olive, sallow, pale, yellow, or ruddy complexions. You will need the same color evaluation skills you learned in the Right Red Discovery Exercise to select these colors. When using your skin color this way, there are no hard-and-fast rules. However, there are some observations and special considerations concerning amount, placement, intensity, and texture that will enable you to effectively use second skin colors.

1. You can use your skin-tone color as part of an outfit, i.e., as a skirt or a jacket; as part of a pattern or design either as the background or foreground color—it could be the thin stripe in a shirt or a wide one in a shawl.
2. The danger of using this color head to toe is that you can look boring or "naked." The amount of your skin-tone color to use in an outfit will be determined by the texture of your skin, the effect you want to create, and the texture of the fabric used. The smoother and more even-toned your complexion the larger the area and the closer to the face it can be. A head-to-toe approach may work just fine for a slinky evening dress—if your body and complexion permit!

3. Be careful about brightness whether from the color or the fabric's shine. It is possible to make your skin look dull next to a too bright version of itself.

Palettes for Pleasure

There is life after work. For many of us, it is our most important life. Focus on whatever makes you feel feminine and sexy, and whatever gets a positive response from the person with whom you share those special times. Do you know what colors turn him on? Find out. Color responses are unique and special. So, while flaming red might hit the mark for some, pink, black, or flesh tones might be in your man's favorite fantasy! Ask and notice how he responds to color. It may require a little experimentation on your part. Have fun. This may be the best kind of "homework" you've done in years. Here are some guidelines:

- Men are partial to warm reds for romantic situations so use peach, true red, and red orange in your clothes, makeup, and surroundings. Pink coral is good for those who look best in cool colors.
- For a more romantic look, use softer, lighter colors from your palette, especially those from the red family. Use these colors in sensual fabrics: satin, silk, cashmere, angora, suede. None of these fabrics are harsh or stiff. They have a pleasing second-skin feel and tend to drape, flow, and subtly accent the body's natural contours. Imagine the look and feel of peach cashmere, pink angora, apricot suede, or rose silk.
- Sexy is different from romantic. It implies a no-pretense-about-what-we-are-up-to level of confidence with brighter tones and sleekness. It is true colors like red, black, emerald green, and metallics rather than pastel tones. It's animal prints rather than florals and leather and suede rather than silk.
- Don't forget to use your imagination and sense of adventure with the colors and patterns you choose for sheets, bedspreads, towels —everything that can affect the mood you want to create.

Full-figured and Fabulous

It has been many years since anyone thought that heavy women should dress in dark colors to make themselves invisible. Now top-notch designers create glamorous fashions for large sizes. It's a diversified market with stores that cater to the mass market and boutiques that have unique high-quality clothes for a discerning clientele. There are fashion magazines and wonderful books detailing dressing strategies for full figures. Heavy women should use their palettes and their preferences, like everyone else, in selecting color. But there is one tool that is especially helpful: color contrast. Wearing several colors rather than one solid color, like a sweater or blazer worn over a contrasting blouse, can help to "break up" the figure. You will often find this principle built into the design of a garment. Diagonal lines are very slimming. Moderate color contrasts are just as effective as high-contrast combinations. Keep your brightest accents near areas of your face and body you want to highlight.

For "Blackaholics"

Black is the easiest color to use as a wardrobe unifier. It is a go-with-everything neutral that can pull multiple colors and patterns into a coherent look and it can be the perfect foil for jewelry. Although the death knell for black as *the* quintessential, always chic fashion color is being sounded, the versatility of black will never go away entirely. It is especially useful if you have a limited budget or if you thrive on an easy, no-fail clothing plan. Black, however, is not flattering to everyone. It can coarsen and gray some complexions and create "warden" effects in others. For diehard "blackaholics," there are ways to use black and to take advantage of its special qualities while controlling its complexion-related liabilities. Try these strategies:

- *Face-off:* Avoid up-to-the-neck black. Wear your best colors around your face or show lots of skin—wear see-through, sheer, or lacy black. Black shoes, bags, skirts, and slacks worn for business, dress, or sportswear can create a coherent color base for other colors and add great flexibility to your wardrobe.
- *Mix it up:* Warm-palette people can add black as a stripe or part of a pattern or weave. It's wonderful with cream, beige, brown, and

olive. Black can also work well with rich pastels (but no black stockings with pastel dresses). It's great in fashion details such as buttons and trim.

- *Lusterize:* Velvets, wool crepes, and rich silks have a gently lustrous quality that is kinder to the skin than the dull and dusty-looking black found in old cotton knits or the brilliant shine of black satin.
- *Accessorize:* Semi-precious stones of onyx or jet, by themselves or set in silver and gold, can add punch to your outfit as can frankly plastic or costume jewelry in black.
- *Be Finicky:* All blacks aren't the same. Some are warmer than others. There are near-black browns and blues that are alternatives to deep black for those who look best in warm colors or who wear the less dramatic cool tones. You'll have to look hard for these colors and train your eye to see the difference.
- *Open up!:* Black isn't the only color that can function as a unifier. According to Margaret Walch, Director of The Color Association of the United States, white is staking out territory as the unifying wardrobe color for a new age. In chapter nine you will learn how to organize a wardrobe around a few well-chosen colors. Open up to rich complex neutrals like eggplant, pine, and wine reds. Even old classics like midnight blue, gray, brown, beige, and olive take on a fresh new look when interestingly coordinated and well accessorized.

Be a Color Collector

Do you ever see a color or color combination in fashion or interior design magazines that fascinates you or makes you feel good? Perhaps you find colors in ribbons or in rocks and shells and glass ground up by the sea? Don't let those experiences slip away! If possible, pick them up, snip them out, or snap them with a camera. Throwing away a favorite but too-worn-out-to-keep towel or blouse? Be sure to keep a piece for the record. Start a color file to keep these samples. Your file can be as simple as an envelope or an old cigar box or as elaborate as a large picture album turned into a swatch book. If you're detail-oriented, you can date samples and indicate why you picked them out. You will be able to use this personal color reference when you need to think about color schemes for your home or decorations for a party. You won't have to depend upon paint store samples. You'll be grateful for this collection because if you're like most people, your memory for color is highly inaccurate. Collecting colors will also give you a way to track your tastes as they change over time.

Color Trends

Just as hemlines go up and down and shoulder pad sizes change, there are trends in color, too. Some seasons you'll find your best colors in fashion and easily available in the stores in a wide range of styles. A season or two later, they're gone or found only in a few clothing items. Color trends are not simply about a particular color, say red, being in and another color, like yellow, being out. They also involve which *qualities* of these colors are in and how colors are put together. Warm reds have recently been hot fashion colors, but not the cool ones. Remember when neon brights were in? Southwest colors? Matte gold? Have you noticed the play of orange and magenta color combinations or subdued neutrals paired with other neutrals? There is always more than one color trend going on. The color story for active sportswear will be different from that for couture or business wear. Learn to spot these trends early by reading fashion magazines—July and August for fall, February and March for spring. With careful wardrobe planning you can stock up on classic styles or that trendy made-for-you item in *your* colors. For those who can't be bothered with the winds and whims of fashion changes, your palette will serve you as a classic color reference.

7 MAKEUP MAGIC

e don't just add color to ourselves with the clothes we wear. We apply color directly to our bodies in the form of cosmetics for our face and hair. Beautification rituals are practiced by all people everywhere. Although their ancient spiritual and social roots are no longer clear to us, there are compelling modern reasons to make the best of our looks. Research proves that positive qualities are attributed to attractive people. They are *assumed* to be smarter, nicer, and even more honest than unattractive people. This phenomenon is known as the "halo effect." In some experiments the same people received significantly higher personality ratings after their hair and makeup was done. Fortunately, an attractive appearance can be achieved regardless of what nature gave us at birth. It makes sense to use flattering clothes in the right colors, a becoming hair style, well-applied makeup, and good grooming habits to become more attractive.

Face First

Makeup helps to define and balance your features, smooth the appearance of your complexion, and minimize the signs of tiredness and time. Women of different life-styles and ages will have varying reasons for using makeup. For the pre-teen, a sheer lip gloss with the slightest hint of color can be a simple and healthy affirmation of her approaching womanhood. Older teens and young adults will experiment as they discover who they are, explore the latest fashions, play with different group identities, and test their individual attractiveness. Working women raising families may want a streamlined beauty routine that doesn't require lots of time. Mature women can look as vital and as young as they feel with the help of makeup.

Today women of color have moved into social, political, and professional arenas we were never before allowed to enter. As entrepreneurs and managers, we now know how critical it is to invest in our image. So, whether you're a CEO or her secretary, a classic polished makeup projects today's business image better than the naked face.

There are more cosmetic options than ever for Black women. You can find a wide range of good products ranging from brands found in discount drugstores to those located exclusively in upscale department stores. A number of exciting cosmetic lines that became available to us within the last five or six years are owned or managed by women of African descent. We also own small independent cosmetic lines that serve a loyal following. Now, even companies that never had suitable colors for the wide range of skin tones found among women of color are showing interest in serving this market. They expect to find that Black isn't just beautiful, it's green with profit.

Makeup as Fashion

Fashions in makeup come and go just as they do in clothing. Sometimes natural or neutral colors are in, at other times the look of the moment is very colorful or dramatic. However, makeup must parallel fashion's attitudes and style. Natural, Classic, Romantic, Dramatic, and Creative are style categories that capture the psychological and image needs of different women. One or two will suit you best, but each style has something to offer you for different occasions in your life. You may save the Dramatic look strictly for Halloween and the Romantic look for your wedding day and never use either again. The spirit of these categories can also support a range of Afrocentric styles—from the use of African jewelry worn with fashionable Western business, casual, or dressy clothes to full African dress. Whatever look you choose, it must be consistent with the style of your clothing and hair. Deep dramatic makeup, sporty clothes, and a conservative hairstyle send an inconsistent and confusing message.

◆ THE NATURAL LOOK This is the look most often requested by African American women. The idea here is to create a natural, healthy glow, not a heavily made-up look, no matter how much makeup you actually use! If foundation is used, it is in the sheerest application possible, covered with a light dusting of powder. For problem complexions, a heavier foundation is necessary. If your complexion is smooth, even toned, and clear, you can use a foundation for special occasions and use powder alone on a daily basis. For this look, blush should be a light to medium skin-tone red that blends easily into your complexion's color and just barely glows on the surface. Use medium to light lipstick shades. If you outline your lips, it should not be visible. Use earth tones and colors that look like an extension of *your* skin. Use matte and soft pearl eye shadows and natural shades of mascara. Avoid complicated techniques, very dark or bright shadows. This look is good for all ages.

◆ THE POLISHED CLASSIC LOOK If you need a conservative, "take charge" business look, this is it. It is similar to the natural look, but has more definition and strength. It requires a softly powdered matte complexion. If blush is used it is understated. Select a medium-toned cream formulation for your lip color, avoid very dark or light colors and lipsticks that are glossy or shiny . Well-shaped brows give strength and definition to your face. Subtly lining your eyes will give them more presence. For eyeshadows, use neutrals like brown, gray, and purple. Select medium red and rose tones for lipsticks in cream and matte formulas. Again, a light hand is required. Avoid the lightest colors—too soft—and the brightest and darkest ones—too dramatic. Remember, an entertainment lawyer who must establish rapport with highly creative people might want a little more drama, which would not be appropriate for the tax lawyer who works with conservative corporate types.

◆ THE ROMANTIC LOOK Think pink, peach, rose. This is the soft side of femininity. For younger women, a soft dewy natural-looking finish to the complexion is appropriate, while the more mature woman should aim for a soft matte complexion. Younger women should use their light and medium palette colors, while mature women should work with their medium shades. Blush is great for this look, as is lipgloss and soft pearl and matte eye shadows in lavenders, grays, and purples rather than earth tones. Use lots of mascara. Blend the colors well; you don't want to see them "sitting" on the skin. Your goal with this look is to maintain a balance between your makeup and the softer colors you're most likely to be wearing. This look is easy to adapt for special-occasion makeup for young girls.

◆ THE DRAMATIC LOOK This is the "Here I am, look at ME" look. You must know who you are and want everyone else to know, too, to carry this off. It's about coming on strong whether you are sexy, trendy, or chic. This look can support strong, bright, or deep colors, strong contrasts, and even exaggeration. You can use a heavier hand in applying your makeup: vibrant lip color, strong eye shaping and definition. But not all at once unless you blend and soften everything to keep from looking overdone and clownish. When you turn the volume up, place the emphasis on either your eyes *or* lips. For evening, you can aim for extremes—a very matte or glittery foundation with matte or glossy lips. If your skin is rough or lined, leave out glittery powder and the extreme matte complexion; create a softer, more natural complexion instead with foundation and powder as described in the natural look.

◆ CREATIVE ARTISTIC LOOK Original and eclectic are some of the words used to describe someone with a personal vision and a sense of style that defies easy categorization. This look is about no rules but *lots* of taste and risk taking. A creative approach to fashion allows you to custom-design an image that positively sets you apart. Your love for one-of-a-kind jewelry, unusual fashion and design, or the unique way you put clothes together have full expression here. Your makeup need not be as exotic—but it should be consistent with your style. You can wear blue lipstick and get away with it if it works as part of the total look.

Your Palette as Makeup Guide

Your palette is an excellent resource for selecting your makeup colors. You don't have to find an exact match. If a cosmetic looks as if it belongs, i.e., coordinates and harmonizes with your other reds, neutrals, lights, brights, and metals, it is probably "in the family" and worth testing on your skin. Some cosmetic companies have their products organized around different complexion undertones. Others divide their products into warm and cool color categories. A few use a more elaborate red, red orange, and yellow undertone system. That's a great help in finding what you need. However, the reds in the color insert and in your palette are your best guide. Here's a warning, though: It is hard to judge how a color will work with your complexion merely by looking at it. Spread some on white tissue or your hand to make the undertone stand out more clearly. For hygienic reasons and for your protection do not use public testers on your face, lips, or eyes. Remember also that department store lighting is notoriously bad for accurately seeing cosmetics. Carry along a hand mirror (one that's not too small) so that you can go outside in natural light to check your color choices.

- Use your dark neutrals and palette colors in the browns, grays, dark greens, blues, and purples as eyeliner, mascara, and contour colors. They give shape, definition, and drama to the eyes.
- Use your Right Reds from light to dark in your lipstick, blushes, and nail color. As blush, they should appear to be an extension—a heightening or deepening—of your natural coloring.
- If you use your brighter colors for eye shadow, do so carefully and use small amounts. In matte and pearl textures these colors act as the colorful counterpoint to the darker colors which give shape and definition to the eyes. Bright shadows are best reserved for evening or dramatic situations. Placing them on the outer third of the eye will keep you from overdoing it. They are also fun colors for mascara.
- Light colors and neutrals like orange, peach, rose, beige, light brown, red violet, and pink which match and blend into your skin can be used all over the eye in matte or soft pearl formulations. Copper and deep gold used sparingly are warm metallic tones which look wonderful on a very wide range of skin tones.
- Select foundations that have the same undertone and depth as your skin color. Test the foundation at the jawline and check the result in natural light to make sure it blends perfectly. You want a color that unifies the colors of your face and neck. Do not use the foundation on your neck.

Palette-by-Palette Suggestions

SAHARA   Easy does it. Your gentle coloring requires moderation. It is easy to get a too-dramatic or a harsh effect with too much brightness or darkness.

SPICE   You can use neutrals very effectively. Your natural coloring demands depth, richness, and definition. Avoid light or dull colors.

BLUES   Your rich dark skin needs medium to deep colors that are thoroughly blended. Avoid cosmetics that are too light, bright, shiny, or ashy and dark, drab lipsticks that dull your complexion.

NILE   A subtle use of color is needed to keep you from looking overdone. Light to medium colors and soft smoky shades look wonderful on you. Avoid very bright or very dark colors.

JAZZ   Dramatic effects work for you. Avoid dull, muted, and light colors. For a more subtle effect use your deep neutrals, matte finishes, and medium colors.

CALYPSO   A certain brightness feels natural for you. Don't wash out your vibrancy with lipstick colors that are too light, dull, or dark. Keep blush colors lively and well blended.

Makeup Mess Ups

- Foundations and powders that are too pink, ashy, or orange for your real skin coloring
- Medium to light blue or green eye shadows used over the whole eye area
- Highly pearlized eye shadow on wrinkled eyelids
- One solid stroke penciled on eyebrows in shades that are too dark, red, or light in comparison to skin and hair tones
- Lipstick and blush colors that are too light or too bright for your depth or coloring and seem to "sit on" or "bounce off" the skin
- Dark lipstick colors that steal the light from the face and dull the complexion
- Highly glossed lips when dressed for business
- Dark, obvious lip liner

- Blush and lipstick in strongly opposing reds, like magenta blush worn with orange lipstick
- Clothes and makeup in strongly opposing reds, like an orange suit and bright magenta lipstick

Matching lipstick, blush, and wardrobe reds is an acceptable approach to putting your colors together. However, using different reds together is more modern, challenging, and exciting. It can be done successfully if the differences are not too great, are easy on the eyes, and allow others to relate to you undistracted by clashing colors on your face and your clothes. Coral and true red can be coordinated with a wide range of other reds. You will have to do your own experimentation to find out what works with your coloring, the makeup you like, and the wardrobe you put together.

Stay current. Over time, changes take place in your skin and body and you will need to make adjustments in the products and colors you use. Don't date yourself by the way you apply your makeup. You can stay fresh and appropriate—at every age—without being faddish.

Learning how to apply makeup well is a practical confidence-building gift to yourself. You can learn from books or magazine articles, or you can take private lessons. If you opt for the latter, select a makeup artist or cosmetician by referral. Look for group makeup lessons in adult education programs. Department store makeup artists are usually excellent. However, "free makeup lesson with purchase" promotions are designed to make you feel good and buy cosmetics rather than to develop your makeup application skills. If you're just learning to work with makeup, look for a private consultation or class in which you get to practice each step of what you are being taught under the direction of a makeup artist or cosmetician.

A good makeup job starts with good skin. Modern cosmetics are beauty enhancers more than camouflagers. The wonderful thing about beauty today is the growing emphasis on its connection to physical and emotional health. That's the real foundation for making a little makeup go a long way.

8 "CROWNING GLORY"

ew things on earth can defy gravity, but our hair is one of them. It can rest on the scalp in happily independent little coils or grow into long, spongy tendrils neatly shaped by hand, or blossom into phantasmagorical forms if left to its own devices. Most of us have some variant of that super-curly form of hair called kinky, although the natural hair texture of Blacks includes curly, wavy, and straight textures. Kinky hair has a reputation for toughness when, in fact, it is extremely fragile. We often think that it's tough because it's resilient enough to withstand heat and strong chemicals that try to make it unnaturally wavy, curly, "bone straight," "peroxide white," golden blonde, oriental blue black, or a rainbow of reds.

Perhaps one of the most hysteria-inducing ideas that ever existed is that hair—rather than brains—is a woman's "crowning glory." But given the market for products dealing with baldness in men, we know women aren't alone in this madness. In fact, hair has been a peculiar obsession of humankind since the beginning of time. It has been the subject of poetry, scholarly research, and even a smash Broadway play and movie called . . . you guessed it: *Hair.* Hair is the stuff of religion, myth, and fairy tales: Samson and Delilah, Rapunzel—and Medusa, whose famous mane of snakes was probably dreadlocks. Some of us believe that hair cutting should be done according to the cycles of the moon, that leaving broken strands of hair in combs or brushes can leave us vulnerable to having "roots" worked on us. People use their hair to display political and religious beliefs, as well as their conformity to or rebellion against what their society considers "proper." During the 1960s, we sprouted mile-high Afros to express that "Black Is Beautiful" and used braids and beads to express a connection to our African roots. Today's "Afro" is a "fade," braids are practically beadless and lengthened with extensions, and cultivated dreadlocks are even colored. Hair is at least as potent as skin color in gauging and reflecting our attitudes about our race-specific characteristics and our culture.

Hair Color

The natural color range for African American hair is jet black through blonde with a wide array of browns and reds in between. While Mother Nature almost always does her job well, more and more women of color are taking matters into their own hands, treating hair color like a cosmetic or fashion accessory. Because of its proximity to your face, the hair color you choose will have a profound effect on the appearance of your complexion. Whether you wish to cover gray, add highlights, enhance your natural color, or make a dramatic or playful statement, color can add new and wonderful dimensions to your look—if it's done well. It is best to have professionals color your hair. They are able to custom-mix colors, add highlights, and mix and blend several shades into your hair to create a more natural or exciting look. As with any professional service, shop around, get referrals, and request a consultation. Not all stylists make good colorists.

There are many different types of hair coloring products available in quality formulas now. So if you want to do it yourself you can. Some products penetrate the hair shaft and others simply coat it, adding volume and shine. There are permanent hair colors, wash-in colors that fade with each shampoo, semi-permanent colors, and those that spray on and wash out in the next shampoo. The one you ultimately select depends on the results you want to achieve, the present condition of your hair, and the chemical processes (straighteners, etc.) you have already used. Read product labels carefully. Follow instructions thoroughly, and do the recommended strand test to see how your hair absorbs the color and whether or not it is weakened by the process. This test is especially critical if your hair has been chemically treated. Be aware that:

- If your hair is fragile and porous it will feel spongy, and may "grab" color so quickly and deeply that you end up with much more color than you expect.
- Different strands of your hair have different textures and may take color differently.
- Dark hair has lots of natural red pigment cells, making it very difficult to eliminate red from the hair.
- Different manufacturers use different color names for similar colors and the same names for widely different ones.

Hair Color Mistakes

Skin and hair colors are complex tones made up of all three primaries—red, yellow, and blue. As discussed in chapter three, "The Skin You're In," a little more red or yellow in a color can affect its warmth or coolness, thereby affecting which skin tones it will flatter. Every day you see women with the wrong hair color because they don't understand how to look at and evaluate colors for themselves. The Right Red Discovery Exercise, learning to see different color qualities—value, undertone, intensity—and finding your palette have given you guidelines for choosing your colors. Think of your hair as you would a garment; if you couldn't *wear* some variation of the color, maybe it shouldn't be surrounding your face! You can avoid the following common hair color mistakes. Alternatives and suggestions are included:

- *Mistake:* Hair color that is too light or too dark for the depth of skin tone.
- *Alternative:* To look natural, choose a tone that is no more than one to two shades lighter than your natural hair color. If you have light skin a three-shade difference *may* be possible. To go darker, also stay within one to two shades of your natural color.
- *Mistake:* The wrong undertone! The most common mistake is the mismatch between the complexion's undertone and the undertone of the chosen hair color. Example: Olive or pink skin with golden blonde or fiery red hair.
- *Alternative:* Try more neutral, i.e., red-brown and blonde tones such as light honey brown with some lighter highlights. Darker olive

complexions can often carry off medium reddish browns rather than lighter shades.

- *Suggestion:* When purchasing a wig or hair for braids or weaves, test them as if they were fabric. Actually hold them up to your face. Reject any that gray your skin, coarsen it, or just seem foreign to your native coloring. Only consider those that look as if they grew out of your skin and brighten and smooth your complexion. When having your hair colored in a salon, review their hair samples using the procedure described above to find a hair sample that the colorist can use to create a new hair color for you.
- *Mistake:* Poorly placed color. Avoid oddly shaped and randomly placed patches of color that do nothing to enhance the shape of your face.
- *Alternative:* Use color strategically. Highlighted areas draw the eyes' attention, so place them to show off pretty eyes or to make a forehead look wider, for example.
- *Mistake:* "Knock 'em dead" hair with "hush-hush" clothes. When bold, dramatic colors such as burgundy, cherry, or fiery red are used as an overall hair color, they demand a total fashion statement to look consistent and appropriate.
- *Alternative:* Use a sheer wash-in product that gives only the slightest suggestion of these dramatic colors, even in sunlight. Both subtle and dramatic variations of these bold tones can be used as strategic highlights rather than as overall color.

Gray Hair

Gray hair provides a lovely natural "back lighting" that softens and brightens your features. That's an extra benefit since many African American women get significant amounts of gray long before their skin shows comparable signs of aging. You can make your gray hair project drama and chic rather than age with a fabulous haircut and stylish clothing in your best colors. If you think your gray is turning drab or yellow, there are salon and at-home products that will enhance your gray. Be sure to get the advice of a trusted professional or friend about how yellow your gray really is. Sometimes, as people age, the cornea of the eye yellows, causing things to appear more yellow than they really are. Avoid old-

◆ HAIR COLOR AND HIGHLIGHT CHART

Palette	Dark	Medium	Light
NILE	WARM BROWN	MEDIUM ASH BROWN	COOL BLONDE–BROWN
	ASH BROWN	VIOLET BROWN	————

Medium dark to medium light browns are best. Avoid strong golden tones.

BLUES	BLACK	————	————
	BLACK BROWN		
	DEEP WARM BROWN		
	BURGUNDY		
	EGGPLANT		

Deep subtle colors are best. Avoid bright, light, and orange shades.

SAHARA	BROWN BLACK	MEDIUM BROWN	LIGHT BROWN
	DEEP WARM BROWN	AUBURN	WARM BLONDE–BROWN

Medium to moderately light warm tones are best. Avoid very bright tones.

SPICE	DEEP WARM BROWN	AUBURN	————
	BROWN BLACK	FIERY AUBURN	

Deep and vibrant rich, warm colors are best. Avoid very light tones.

JAZZ	BROWN BLACK	WARM BROWN	————
	BURGUNDY	CHERRY	
	EGGPLANT	BROWNISH AUBURN	
	BLACK		

Deep rich and vibrant cool tones are best. Avoid light and orange red tones.

CALYPSO	BROWN BLACK	BROWNISH AUBURN	————
	DEEP WARM BROWN	CHERRY	
		AUBURN	

Moderately bright tones are best. Select brown black, deep warm brown, and browned auburn to maximize your ability to wear warm and cool colors.

fashioned products that give the illusion of whitening gray when they actually give you the "blue hair syndrome."

If you prefer to cover your gray, you have a choice between at-home products and the services of a salon. If you have a lot of gray—over 30 percent—a salon can create greater subtlety and variety more easily than you can at home. However, the same advice and cautions noted in the "Hair Color" section above apply here as well. Your challenge will be to avoid the harshness of a too-dark color and the brassy or unnatural-looking results from tones that are too bright, light, or too red.

Gray hair presents as much of a color challenge as any other color. Some grays are brilliantly white, others are soft white, and still others appear slightly warm. Most shades of gray hair blend easily with the cool, blue-based palettes of Jazz and Blues and Nile. Will you need to change your clothing colors as your hair turns gray? If you belong to the Nile palette, no. If you belong to a palette full of very vibrant colors like Jazz or Blues, you may find yourself naturally shifting to lighter and less intense versions of your colors and saving the brightest ones for accents. This does not mean dull or pastel, especially if you have a strong physical presence. The Right Red Discovery Exercise and the experience you'll receive over the years picking good-for-you colors will train you to see any need for change.

Cool Hair and Warm Palettes

Warm palette people face additional challenges. If you have significant amounts of gray (40 percent or more) and you look best in the warm Spice and Sahara palettes, you will want to shift some of your warmest colors to more neutral, i.e., less warm, tones. It is mostly your white, beige, and light brown colors that are affected. The more gray you have, the more of an issue it is. For example, if beige has been a color that you enjoy, stay with it. But select less yellow and more neutral beige tones. Rather than buying a camel-colored jacket, get one with less yellow undertones like stone or warm taupe as long as it works with your complexion. Check your whites to make sure that they appear related to your hair rather than in opposition to it. Neutral whites—off-white, soft white, and slightly warm whites like eggshell—will harmonize with your hair and your skin more readily than very yellow whites like butter cream. You'll create a very lovely frame around you when the white tones of your hair and wardrobe work together. Use the Right Red Discovery process with different whites and beiges to carefully evaluate the effect of these shades as your hair color changes.

A Cut Above

A wonderful hairstyle is a result of its shape, color, and texture working together in a way that makes you look good. Your hair sets the tone for your look. Some Black women behave as if they've been asked to give up their firstborn child when a stylist suggests they cut off one millimeter of hair. They are willing to hang on to style-defeating split and straggling ends, choosing the illusion of quantity over quality. Sometimes a dramatic color is chosen for hair that has no real shape or style, as if the color alone can make a statement. A haircut is like the frame and foundation of a house. The better the construction and design, the better it will look and the longer it will last. And the better you look.

Black and Blonde:
Should She or Shouldn't She?

The concept of the "American blonde"—preferably blue-eyed—has been used as a measure of beauty to bully women of every race and ethnic background. It is the antithesis of the beauty that is most common to people around the world and to people of African descent in particular. Yet there are more than a few women of color who seem to buy into the concept that "blondes have more fun" by donning blonde wigs and hair extensions, and pouring on the color. More often than not the resultant hair colors clash with their natural coloring and detract from their real beauty. Rarely does blonde hair complement medium to dark complexions. The hair usually looks too brassy, bright, or golden for the skin and complexion flaws are exaggerated. Light and olive skin tones can be coarsened, grayed, or made more olive by contrast. Our most beautifying colors, based on our real complexion qualities, are made less effective because they clash with the artificial hair color. Some women of color, however, use blonde coloring in ways that seem to extend and celebrate their natural coloring. The results can be stunning and unique. The contrast of just the right blonde tone against dark skin is unique and dramatic when supported by an equally striking fashion statement.

This kind of "going for the gold" raises more than cosmetic considerations. Is fashion a front for low self-esteem or racial self-hatred? Should every alteration of our natural attributes be questioned in this way? Is a Black woman wearing blonde hair more significant than a dark Italian going blonde or an Asian woman perming her naturally straight hair?

Perhaps not. It is possible to treat our skin color as a lovely canvas to be decorated with appropriately beautifying colors. Therefore, the right shade of blonde hair and blue or green contact lenses can indeed be worn to create an "interesting" or "exotic" look. But we must never forget that our color is also tied to an ancient heritage and culture that is precious and irreplaceable. We can use our personal fashion and beauty decisions to support our belief in our heritage. We should never allow the technology of what is available—chemically induced blonde hair and colored contact lenses, for example—to take us where our consciousness would not. That is not to suggest that there is only one correct approach. There are many. But only consider options that reflect and increase your self-worth and value who you are—roots, personal quirks, dreams, and all.

As we approach the twenty-first century, we will be more stylistically diversified than ever before. Those of us who have difficulty seeing and honoring the beauty in African characteristics would do well to explore such feelings—gently and without accusation—and to open themselves up to a wider, richer, and more self-sustaining definition of beauty. It is in our self-interest to embrace our own diversity.

9 PLAYING WITH COLOR

o you admire the way designers and fashion magazines coordinate outfits with beautiful and sometimes daring color combinations? Are you totally mystified about how to do this for yourself? Many women would love to be more adventurous with color, but don't quite know which colors can be worn together. In this chapter you will learn techniques that will make these decisions easier. Sensitivity to yourself is also essential to creating a wardrobe that looks and feels the way you want it to. Just as you have a preference for one color over another, you have a preference for some color combinations. Look in your closet, your personal color philosophy is there. Is it "the more the merrier" or is it closer to "moderation is the key"? Let's start where you are now before we begin to explore new possibilities. Which one of these Personal Color Profiles describes you?

- *Intuitive and expressive.* You know precisely what you like and what feels good to you; other opinions don't matter. If you hate red, no matter what anyone says, you won't go near it. Love purple? Whether in or out of fashion, it's your color. You love certain combinations and are totally indifferent to others. Your feelings are strong and you have the courage of your convictions.
- *Better safe than sorry.* You know that white blouses and classic neutrals like navy, beige, and gray can be worn with most every-

thing. You may actually enjoy color, but feel inhibited about creating a more colorful image.

- **Fashion focused.** If it's in, you're in it. You enjoy the change and challenge of fashion. If your knees or hips aren't quite what they should be for a particular style, you refuse to notice. You are sure that you can wear every color. You enjoy participating in the energy that surrounds whatever is the "latest."
- **Color happy.** There is a rainbow in your closet. You love color and everybody knows it. You relate to the energy that color gives you, your surroundings, and other people. Although you have a lot of color variety, you may have less clothing flexibility because creating workable outfits from many colors can be difficult.

Maybe your profile is a variant of one of these, or a combination of a few of these themes. Any of these profiles is a good place to start being more adventurous with color. That doesn't mean working with a lot more color necessarily, but it does mean working with color in new and different ways. You will have an opportunity to explore various tried-and-true color combinations and to decide which ones attract you the most. Breaking into new color territory can be enjoyable and can take different forms.

◆ VISUAL EXPERIMENTATION One way to break your color gridlock is to throw everything onto the bed and *see* what color relationships show up! See what pleases your eye, even if it seems unusual and you've never seen it before. Try to put your clothes together without prejudice. The wardrobe wheel exercise on page 104 gives you a systematic approach to finding new clothing and color relationships. You have everything you need to get started: a bed and your clothes! Any of your newly matched outfits that seem "iffy" can be hung on a hanger—arranged just the way you would wear them. Look at them for a few days and make adjustments and decisions about how they look.

◆ ANCESTRAL TRADITIONS Mixing patterns and putting together many different colors is part of the African and Caribbean tradition. Don't wait for European designers to introduce their interpretations of "ethnic style" into mainstream fashion. It's a concept you can already claim; it's part of your heritage. There are many wonderful books on African and Caribbean art and design. Study them. Visit museums where our heritage is displayed and be inspired by what you see. Keeping the print and pattern focus in mind, use the same visual experimental approach described above. We may no longer be in intimate contact with the great spiritual and social symbolism found in African color and design, but, as children of Africa, no matter how far away or how long displaced, surely the motherland resonates somewhere within.

♦ CLASSIC/SYSTEMATIC This approach uses tools like the color wheel as guides to putting colors together. I used one based on the Munsell color wheel format. The color wheel is a circle of colors organized in a strict order that allows you to keep track of color relationships with mathematical precision. For example, triadic color relationship is three harmonious colors spaced at equal distances from each other around the wheel. In fact, if a point were placed in the center of each color and the points were joined by straight lines, the lines would form an equilateral triangle. Turn that triangle like a dial to any other set of colors on the wheel and you still have a harmonious triadic relationship. That's the magic and beauty of this instrument. While it makes some of the decisions about hue for you, you have many more decisions to make regarding the other color qualities —value, intensity, and undertone—as well as how much of each color to use.

Color Strategy

Color relationships are a little like dance relationships. Some, like today's "voguing," are solo affairs. Others, like the waltz, mambo, or lindy, require a partner. Old-time folk dances use groups of people doing segments in threes, fours, and fives. Whatever number of colors used, the goal is to create harmony—some form of pleasing visual unity between the colors, the clothes, and you. The color schemes that follow are based on the use of the color wheel that you will find in the color insert.

Equally important to the experience of harmony is proportion, or the amount of each color that is used. As a general guide, one color should dominate the outfit, a second or subordinate color should be used in a moderate amount, and the third color—if there is one—should be a minor accent. You see this every day—a suit's color dominates an outfit, the blouse is the second color, clearly taking up less visual space than the suit. A scarf or pocket square could carry a third color, used sparingly. Even when only two colors are being used, it is much more interesting to select one as the dominant color. There are basically three kinds of harmonious color schemes: those based on a similarity of qualities, those based on a contrast of qualities, and those that unite colors using both similarity and contrast.

Harmonies Based on Similarity

Monochromatic and analogous color schemes use a strong family resemblance between colors to create harmony. Each one has something to offer you as you try to project your personality and meet the requirements of your job and social life.

◆ MONOCHROMATIC COLOR SCHEMES These are soloists. One color is used alone or in several light to dark shades. This is the head-to-toe approach of the all-black or all-purple outfit and also of combinations like chocolate, beige, and tan. This is a wonderful look when pattern and texture are used to create variety. A monochromatic gray outfit becomes visually interesting when it consists of deep gray wool slacks with a dark and light striped gray jacket. These stripes create the effect of a medium gray without the flatness of the solid color. A pearl gray jacquard blouse could complete the outfit.

The character of the single color or the shades of that color dictate the psychological impact of the outfit. An all-pink outfit suggests femininity and softness, all red would project energy and force, while shades of brown suggest an approachable, conservative person.

◆ ANALOGOUS COLOR SCHEMES This group of harmonies relies on an almost "peas in the pod" family resemblance. The appeal and harmony of these colors is the close visual resemblance of the group members, like a five-part-harmony singing group. Traditionally analogous colors are the ones that lie next to each other on the color wheel—a primary or secondary color and the two colors on either side of it:

Jazz Palette

Erica

Erica's rich and vibrant coffee brown complexion lights up when surrounded by the high energy, mostly cool colors of the Jazz palette. Her deep complexion and dark hair and eyes allow her to "stand up" to such dramatic color contrasts as this red suit accented with a bold black and white print scarf.

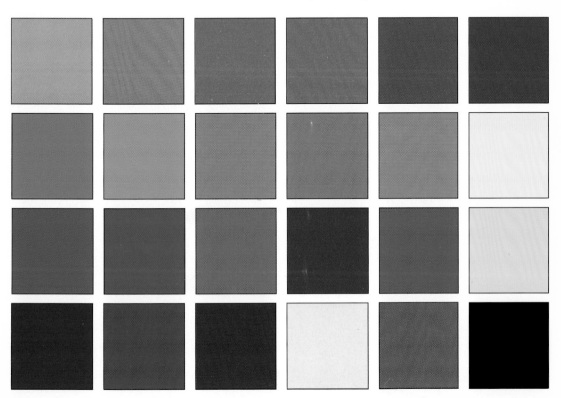

Spice Palette

Chey

Chey's bright warm complexion and fiery auburn hair are an exquisite match for the piquant quality of the Spice palette colors. For this artist-designer a creative, high voltage look works wonders.

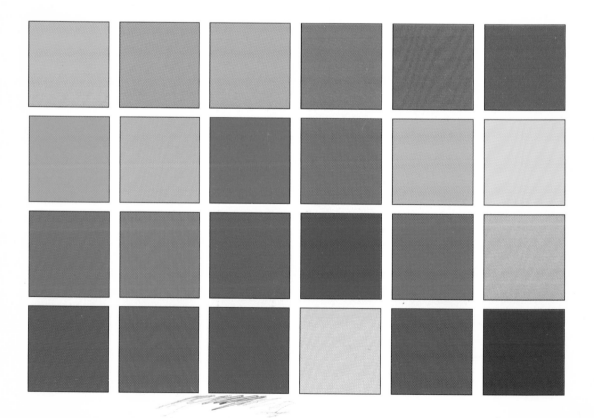

Blues Palette

Cyndee

Cyndee's rich ebony skin glows against regal full-of-presence colors found in the Blues palette. Her flowing pearl gray jacket makes a beautiful background for her coloring. The dramatic scale of the black and white polka dot scarf shows how an all-neutral outfit can have great flair.

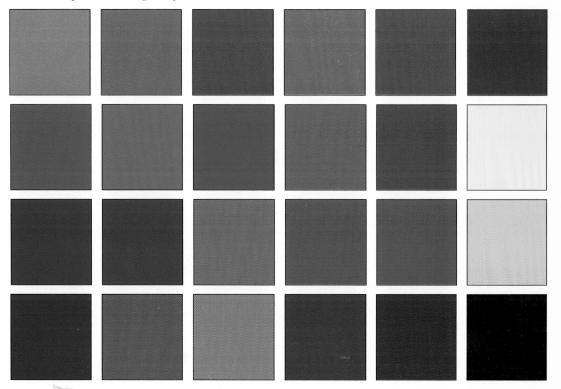

Sahara Palette

Cay

Cay's light golden skin and dark honey brown hair resonate beautifully with Sahara's clear warm colors. Her light cinnamon suit and blue print scarf provide a wonderfully polished professional look without the use of traditional or dark business colors.

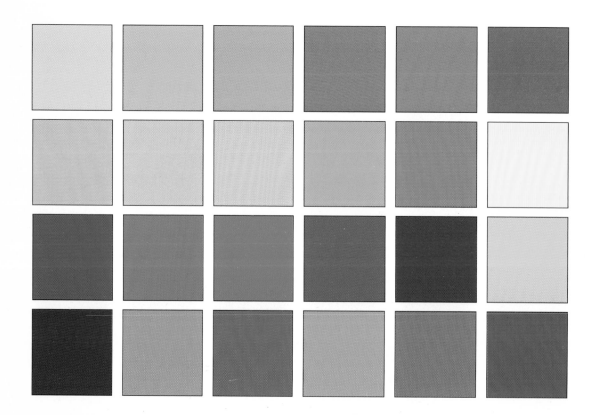

Calypso Palette

Pansy

Pansy's deep creamy chocolate complexion is a "color magnet" that responds beautifully to a very wide range of warm and cool colors. Her simple two-color outfit combines a deep cool black and a rich warm mustard with stunning results.

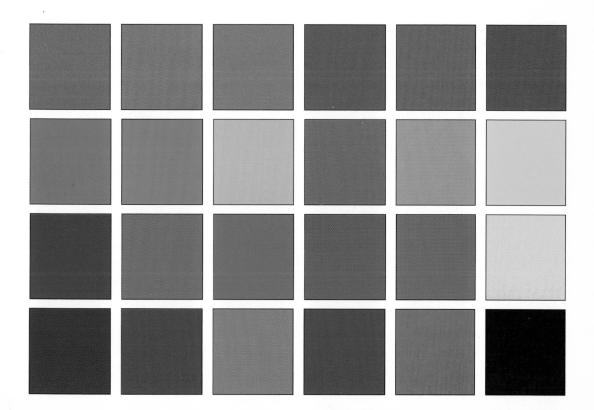

Family Differences

Cynthia

Arsha

Donna

Diane

It is very common in our families to have a rainbow of skin tones. Each family member must make individual choices to decide on her best colors.

Cynthia and Arsha are a beautiful mother and daughter duo with coloring close enough to have many similarities between their best colors yet have many differences as well. Cynthia takes her cue from the mostly cool Jazz palette; Arsha's complexion takes warm and cool colors. That makes her a Calypso.

Donna and Diane are sisters who share a lot in life but not when it comes to wardrobe or cosmetic colors. Donna's best colors are warm and clear and found in Sahara. Diane lights up in Jazz which is cool, bright and darker in tone.

Cheryl's beautiful response to Nile colors (see insert page 2) makes her an ideal representative of that unique group of those with ash, rose, and pink undertones.

Red Chart

Which group of reds looks best on you? Use the Red Chart as a guide in selecting color samples to test next to your face. See the Right Red Discovery Exercise in Chapter 4.

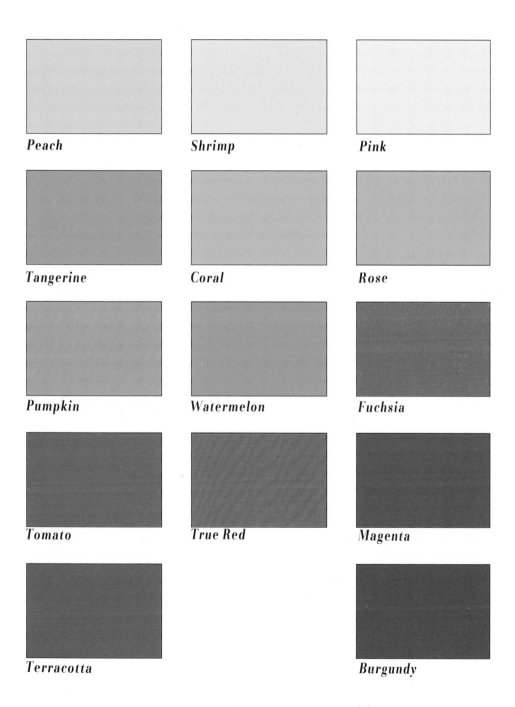

Peach	Shrimp	Pink
Tangerine	Coral	Rose
Pumpkin	Watermelon	Fuchsia
Tomato	True Red	Magenta
Terracotta		Burgundy

Nile Palette

Cheryl

Cheryl's beige pink skin and dark ash brown hair are set off beautifully with the cool clear tones of the Nile palette. Her lavender pink suit accented with an amethyst and blue scarf have a soft and lively quality. Very dark or very bright colors would overwhelm the gentleness of her natural coloring.

A Blues Extended Family

Patricia

Cyndee

Patricia's deep vibrant complexion responds beautifully to the deep subtle richness of the Blues palette. Her medium-toned softly muted magenta suit with a multi-toned blouse of related colors is accessorized by black and crystal accessories. The look is stylish and sophisticated. One of her favorite outfits is this dressy and feminine light pink dress. The high contrast between its color and her skin beautifully deepens the appearance of her complexion. It is made more dramatic by her polished silver jewelry.

A Sahara Extended Family

Donna

Candy

Cay

Candy and Donna fit into this palette though their coloring is somewhat different than Cay's. They both have light warm complexions. Candy has deep olive green eyes, dark auburn brown hair, and light red brown freckles. She wears the richer tones of the Sahara palette and some of the softer Spice tones. Her leaf pattern shirt makes a perfect sporty look that highlights her coloring. Donna's complexion is ivory. Her naturally sandy brown hair has blonde highlights. Donna avoids the orange tones in her palette in favor of corals and warm roses. Her personality demands some colors that have a dramatic effect such as this tomato red suit which looks fabulous on her.

A Spice Extended Family

Esther

Chey

Esther does double duty as our addition to the Spice palette. You can see how the creamy white satin and marigold silk evening suit beautifully both contrasts and reflects the natural tones in her complexion, hair, and eyes. Esther's coloring responds especially well to the "rich fire" in colors like this deep teal blouse. Dull or light colors would steal her vibrant quality.

A Jazz Extended Family

Nancy

Cynthia

Erica

Diane

Lenore

A wide range of light to dark skins sparkle with the jewel bright colors of the Jazz palette. Nancy's olive complexion, dark hair, and eyes are bright and glowing against her indigo and white African dress. Cynthia looks stunning in this dramatic green and purple combination. Black and white never looked better than it does on Erica. Diane's red brown skin tone is vibrant against the fuchsia suit accented with black and silver. Lenore's cool yellow complexion looks wonderful next to her magenta blouse topped by a print jacket of taupe, white, cool blue and green accented with a few warm tones.

A Calypso Extended Family

Arsha

Sheana

Pansy

Arsha's vibrant golden red brown skin gives her a wide range of warm and cool color choices from the Calypso palette. Sheana's olive-ivory complexion and dark hair and eyes allow her to wear vibrant colors. Her silk dress is a lively sophisticated blend of warm and cool shades.

A Cool Woman Gone Warm

Sheila

Sheila belongs to the Jazz palette. She looks radiant in her electric blue suit and scarf. But she is also attracted to lots of warm colors. Her stylish mustard suit is a case in point. The mustard color is too similar to her complexion and its warm undertone competes with the cool yellow in her skin. She employs a scarf as a color bridge to bring more flattering colors next to her face. In the picture on the right, she uses a scarf with favorite warm colors dominated by green, orange, and coral accented with cool purple. Although her complexion appears slightly less radiant, these warm and vivacious colors make her feel good. On the left she wears a scarf of rich blue and red neutrals with cool undertones interwoven with a dark mustard. It covers a lot more of the jacket than in the picture on the right. Because the value level and tone of this scarf is similar to that of her hair it makes a lovely frame for her face. It's a refined and serious image lightened by the dangling earrings.

This warm-cool strategy is natural for people who wear Calypso's colors. If you belong to a warm palette and you are fond of certain cool colors, reverse this strategy. Use the system you learned in the Right Red Discovery Exercise to determine how far you can go with favorite colors in your opposite undertone.

Makeup Magic

These pictures speak for themselves. Using their palettes as a guide, these naturally lovely ladies have added polish and pizazz to their looks with makeup in their best colors.

Color Wheel

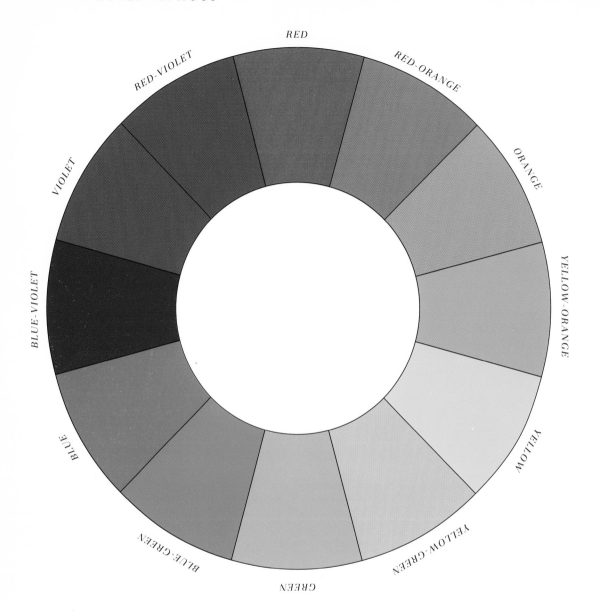

◆ ANALOGOUS COLOR SCHEMES

RED VIOLET	RED	RED ORANGE
YELLOW ORANGE	YELLOW	YELLOW GREEN
BLUE GREEN	BLUE	BLUE VIOLET
RED ORANGE	ORANGE	YELLOW ORANGE
YELLOW GREEN	GREEN	BLUE GREEN
RED VIOLET	VIOLET	BLUE VIOLET

Such combinations provide more variety and contrast than monochromatic color schemes. Analogous colors are easiest to work with when the intensity of each color is similar. However, intensity changes in an outfit that follows the dominant-subordinate-minor note ratio can be very pleasing, i.e., a bright violet dress can be paired with a short blue violet sequined jacket and a muted red violet scarf.

𝓗𝒶𝓇𝓂𝑜𝓃𝒾𝑒𝓈 𝓑𝒶𝓈𝑒𝒹 𝑜𝓃 𝓒𝑜𝓃𝓉𝓇𝒶𝓈𝓉

Contrasting colors suggest tension, excitement, fun, and energy when they are bright; sophistication and refinement when muted.

◆ COMPLEMENTARY COLOR SCHEMES These are based on an exclusive pair of colors that are directly opposite each other on the color wheel. You can draw a straight line from one to the other. One is always warm and the other cool.

When thinking about putting colors together, remember that every color is available in a wide range of shades from light to dark, bright to dull. For instance, when the complementary pair red and green come to mind, do you think exclusively of Christmas? Red and green could also be pale pink and deep pine; rose and pea soup green; or olive and maroon. And there are still many more possibilities to consider!

To use this color scheme effectively, balance the contrast of the colors by value (lightness/darkness) and intensity (brightness/dullness). A light rose-colored scarf and a sage green summer suit both have medium lightness and a soft muted quality. Equally effective but very different in impact would be a bright scarlet evening suit accented by a sheer,

◆ COMPLEMENTARY COLOR SCHEMES

Warm	Cool
RED	GREEN
RED ORANGE	BLUE GREEN
YELLOW	VIOLET
YELLOW GREEN	RED VIOLET
ORANGE	BLUE
YELLOW ORANGE	BLUE VIOLET

shimmering silk chiffon scarf in moss green. Again, in each of these schemes one color is clearly subordinate.

◆ TRIADIC COLOR SCHEMES These harmonies do a lively three-member dance in which each member of the trio is a strong individual performer. The most obvious triadic color groups are made up of the primaries and secondaries.

◆ TRIADIC COLOR SCHEMES

RED	BLUE	YELLOW
ORANGE	GREEN	VIOLET
RED ORANGE	YELLOW GREEN	BLUE VIOLET
YELLOW ORANGE	BLUE GREEN	RED VIOLET

Simple, direct combinations like red, blue, and yellow are playful and energetic, making them ideal choices for children's products and sportswear. These trios can be made more interesting and sophisticated when the colors are muted. Imagine the impact of a dark blue violet jumpsuit combined with a brick (a browned red orange) suede jacket, accented by a bright yellow green scarf tucked into the neckline. And what about olive green slacks and matching sweater with a scarf that has a peach and purple floral design on a black background?

Harmonies of Contrast and Similarity

♦ SPLIT-COMPLEMENTS These perform an intricate three-way dance involving analogous and complementary colors. A split complement is formed by a primary or secondary and the two analogous colors on either side of its complementary color:

♦ SPLIT-COMPLEMENT COLOR SCHEMES

RED	YELLOW GREEN	BLUE GREEN
YELLOW	BLUE VIOLET	RED VIOLET
BLUE	RED ORANGE	YELLOW ORANGE
ORANGE	BLUE GREEN	BLUE VIOLET
GREEN	RED VIOLET	RED ORANGE
VIOLET	YELLOW ORANGE	YELLOW GREEN

Imagine a muted buttercup yellow cardigan over a beautiful dress in blue violet tones that is belted in deep red violet suede.

Color Schemes and Your Palette

Every palette can take advantage of these coordination strategies. Monochromatic schemes are easy—just pick your best color or a neutral that you like. Analogous color schemes let you stay all warm or all cool. In complementary, triadic, and split-complement color schemes involving warm and cool colors, select the largest proportion, the brightest tones, and the colors that will be closest to your face among your palette colors. Conversely, use the colors with the undertones not found in your palette as accent colors, in subdued tones, and away from your face.

Neutrals: Everybody's Partner

Neutrals have a reputation for being everybody's partner. Black, white, and gray are the quintessential go-with-everything neutrals, while beige, brown, and navy have more limited applications. We use them as the workhorse colors of our wardrobes. They show off other colors by acting as a background: a navy dress with a colorful scarf or a dark suit with a great piece of jewelry. A neutral background can also unify several colors that would otherwise look garish or unconnected.

Neutrals aren't always as "neutral" as they appear. Some blacks appear denser and blacker than others or contain hints of other tones. Grays can have a blue, mauve, or even greenish cast. Some beiges are more yellow than others and navy can have a hint of purple, making it resemble blueberry, or it can have enough black in it to be called midnight. Brown can have red, yellow, or gray undertones. These subtleties are important since they affect how well the neutral you've selected will blend with your colors.

There are colorful neutrals that have less versatility than black, gray, and navy. Instead, they offer richness and character: deep wine reds, blackened greens, olive, and rich purples and red violets. Even colors such as orange and yellow when muted and bronzed, i.e., made more neutral, become more versatile.

Neutrals are perfect in monochromatic color schemes or in combination with other neutrals, e.g., navy and white or navy, gray, and tan. Neutrals are wonderful with color. One strategy is to wear a wildly (or mildly) multicolored item like a scarf or jacket with a solid neutral outfit. Then there is the one-shot strategy of adding a stunning piece of jewelry or one striking color to an all-neutral background: a black dress with a bright red silk lapel rose or a white pantsuit with a flowing teal scarf.

This overview and sampling of color relationships in no way exhausts the possibilities of color harmony even within the wheel. There are effective approaches to combining colors that defy categorization by this method. Be inspired by color combinations seen in art or found in nature. This tour will, I hope, demystify it a little and inspire you to really play with color.

10 WARDROBE WORKOUT

o you have a closet full of clothes and nothing to wear? Do you have blouses that only look good with one or two suits and other blouses that don't really work with anything? Looking wonderful has little to do with the number and variety of individual clothing items you own and everything to do with how beautifully they work together to create all the outfits you need —every day, for every occasion. That's the difference between a really great wardrobe and a collection of clothes. Your wardrobe should provide you with *complete* outfits. Complete means head to toe and inside out, with outer wear: coats, jackets, raincoats; lingerie; basic items: dresses, suits, skirts, pants, jeans, sweatsuits, sweaters, blouses; and accessories: shoes, bags, jewelry, hats, gloves, scarves, hair ornaments.

A well-functioning wardrobe provides you with garments and accessories in which the styles, colors, and textures enhance your complexion, flatter your figure, and make you feel good about being you. Each item should be related to the whole so that it coordinates easily with everything else. At the same time, there should be enough variety to keep your wardrobe interesting. The "ideal" wardrobe is defined by your particular needs. An artist, a student, a corporate officer, or a postal employee who wears a uniform every day may have very different requirements.

Planning a wardrobe requires:

- An image goal, i.e., a definite image or style that you want to project
- A shopping plan, i.e., a list of items that you want, specified by color and style
- An assessment of what you now have

The purpose of this chapter is to give you a systematic and organized approach to developing your wardrobe. It *is* a workout, but it will be fun to go through these wardrobe evaluation and planning exercises. You will know what you have that works, what you need to get rid of, and what you need to keep to create the wardrobe that you want.

Read the whole chapter first. Then go back and go through the suggested exercises. You will need to schedule time, perhaps over several weekends, to do a thorough job. Worksheets have been included. So, roll up your sleeves. This section will move you from the *idea* of having good outfits coming out of your closet every day to the *reality*.

Image Goals

Making decisions about what to keep, what to discard, and what to add is easier if you have an image of how you want to look. To be Earth Mother one minute and chic and elegant the next puts serious strains on a wardrobe. We all have many facets of ourselves that bring richness to our lives, but there will be some consistent themes. You can become more aware of what you like by making a clipping file of pictures showing colors and styles that attract you. Do not shortchange this process by being cautious and editing out looks that you really like but are afraid of "at your age," or "in your size." Let yourself experience what you like without limitations. Learn from these pictures. Collect enough and you will start to see a pattern in what attracts you. Notice shapes, proportions, and textures of what you like. Develop a list of descriptive words that reinforces this image in your mind. And, develop a list of opposite qualities that you want to avoid. Your "Love It" list could read like this: elegant, couture designs, subtle but rich colors, excellent fabric, expensive jewelry. Your "Not Me" list could have: pastels, corporate navy, and gray. Or your "Love It" list could be: sexy, glamorous, feminine drapy fabric, body-conscious fit to clothes. "Not Me" might be: heavy fabric, boxy shapes, dull colors. Be sure to notice hairstyles and accessories you like. It's an opportunity to become clear on what *you* want for you.

Having a vision of how you want to look—a vision that is authentic to your body and soul—and then translating that vision into a personal style with the color and design of your clothes, accessories, hair, and makeup, is a worthy adventure in self-development and self-expression.

The Life-style Audit

Completing your life-style audit will enable you to see how well your wardrobe serves your needs, where there are missing items or overabundance. Looking at all these points will help to bring your wardrobe into line with your real-life requirements.

Use the Life-style Audit chart below. List under "Activity" the areas of your life that need different kinds of clothes: work, leisure time, sports, or working out, for example. If you have a job in which casual clothes, the kind you would also wear during off-hours, are acceptable, be sure to list both activities anyway. Determine the total number of hours per week you usually spend in each activity and then figure out the time spent in each activity as a percentage of the total time you have available. You have 119 available hours: 24 hours × 7 days = 168 hours, minus 49 hours of sleep per week = 119 available hours.

Once you've done that, you then have a picture of the activities for which you need different clothes. It would be easy to decide that the area that involves most of your time merits the greatest wardrobe investment. That would be true if that area is also a priority for you. What if you have a nine-to-five job that doesn't demand an expensive wardrobe, and you have a second career as a nightclub entertainer that requires glitzy things? You may perform only once or twice a month, but each show has the potential to propel you into the career of your dreams. As a result, you may choose to invest more heavily in this important part of your life even though it involves less time than your nine-to-five job. What about those non-priority areas that require a lot of your time? Don't spend more money than necessary here and end up with less money available for the activities you really care about. Don't undermine your image—to yourself or others—by inappropriately under-investing in your most important clothes. You have to look like a star before you are one! Use these wardrobe plans to help you build attractive groups of clothes so you can look good for all your activities without buying the store.

◆ LIFE-STYLE AUDIT

Assign the letter A to all activities with a high priority for you, the letter B to important activities, and the letter C to those unimportant but necessary activities which, if you could, you would eliminate from your life.

Activity	Priority	Number of Hours/ Percentage of Time
1.		
2.		
3.		
4.		
5.		
6.		

The Closet Audit

Now that you are clear about the kinds of activities your clothes need to serve, it's time to make room for new clothes by getting rid of the dead wood in your closet. Weed out:

- Things you hate (even if they're expensive)
- Things that don't fit (and can't be altered)
- Unflattering colors and patterns
- Really old-fashioned styles
- Stained and irreparable items

Don't feel obliged to discard anything you love because the color isn't perfect for you. Place those garments in a separate pile and refer to chapter nine, "Playing with Color," to see how you can wear them with other colors and accessories.

After this process, what's left are effective, useful garments that can be repaired or altered if needed. They have passed with flying colors your clothing criteria for color, style, fit, and emotional appeal.

These clothes form your *Current Wardrobe Core.* Separate business clothes from sportswear, etc. You need to see how you are covered in each activity. You will develop your full wardrobe from this base. Even if you have very few items in categories that are most important to you, it is much better to start with a solid group of clothes that make you feel good and truly represent who you are today than lots of "stuff" that doesn't work.

Lessons from the "Junk Pile"

Conducting a personal clothing inventory is like being your own anthropologist and psychologist on the one hand and a demolition expert and designer on the other. The process of weeding out garments can be very self-confrontational. You might have to face the diets you've failed, money wasted, and the body parts that won't conform to your ideals. But there are pleasant aspects of this process as well: the memory of special occasions, those items that always get you compliments, and those outfits that "knocked them dead." And what about those always-works-no-matter-what clothes that you wear until they're rags, when you reluctantly and finally say good-bye as if to old friends? There's a lot of history in your old clothes.

Take a good look at the differences between what you've decided to keep and what you plan to discard. Is your junk pile full of clothes with patterns that now seem too busy or colors that are too dull or every ruffled item you thought would make you look "more feminine"? Were you attracted to certain styles because a friend or someone whose image you admire wears them successfully? By simply looking at the two piles of clothes, the differences between them should stand out clearly. If not, the following exercise will help you take a closer look. Both piles will help you sharpen your self-image goals.

◆ JUNK PILE EVALUATION FORM

For each of the design factors, compare the difference between the clothes that work for you and those that don't.

Design Factor	Rejected Clothes	Effective Clothes
Color		
Fabric		
Pattern		
Style		
Other Observations		

But What Do I Do Tomorrow Morning?

Even when money is no barrier, developing a wardrobe takes time. In fact, two to three shopping seasons (two springs and two winters) is reasonable. But what do you do in the interim? Especially after you've purged your wardrobe. Go shopping in your closet for overlooked outfits. How do you find them? The following technique is based on the wardrobe wheel concept. It was developed by two home economists, Jeane Johnson and Anne Foster, in their textbook, *Clothing Impact and Image.* It is a more systematic approach to the visual experimental "throw it on the bed" method.

- Take a basic clothing item like a skirt or a matched suit from your Current Wardrobe Core (treat a suit as a single item) and place it on the bed.
- Try every blouse and sweater from your Wardrobe Core to see what coordinates with it. Place the ones that do in a circle around the skirt or suit.
- Around each blouse, add accessories that give you a finished look: shoes, bags, jewelry, scarves, etc. While all the outfits may share the same shoes and bags, the jewelry and scarves can change to accommodate the different colors or styles in the blouses.

You have just identified all the outfits your current wardrobe will provide with that suit. Any surprises? Repeat the process with all suits, all skirts, and pants, using all the blouses and sweaters again. You don't have to have suits to make use of this process. Every kind of wardrobe can be accommodated by this technique. If you wear mostly sweaters, shirts or blouses, and slacks, it will still work:

- Make a skirt the centerpiece.
- See how many blouses (turtlenecks, T-shirts, pullovers) coordinate with it.
- Then see how many cardigans or knit sweaters work with the different blouse-skirt combinations.
- Now repeat the process for all your skirts and slacks.

If you're like most people, you get used to wearing your clothes one way. This exercise gives you an opportunity to find new outfits, to explore new and more interesting ways to put your clothes together, and to include new and different color combinations. You may find lots of things to wear. Even if they are not exactly the look you want now, remember you are buying time to create the wardrobe that you do want.

The Anatomy of a Wardrobe

With image goals in mind, a wardrobe core to build on, and a cleaned-out closet, let's look at what is required to create the wardrobe of your dreams. We'll start by looking at the mechanics or basic components of a wardrobe. This will provide you with a road map to the process of building one.

All wardrobes share these basic components. How they are filled in will vary according to the life-style of each person. A wardrobe has three parts:

1. *Major Pieces.* These are the workhorse items. They are worn frequently, must last many seasons, and often require a substantial investment compared to other wardrobe items. They usually include coats, jackets, suits, blazers, and dresses. Although the following items are usually listed under accessories, escalating costs now place them in this category: gold jewelry, and fine leather shoes and bags. The

colors selected for these items set the tones for the rest of the wardrobe.

2. *Support Pieces.* These items provide color and variety to your wardrobe: blouses, sweaters. Their colors must support and coordinate with those of the major pieces.

3. *Accessories.* This group includes scarves, belts, costume jewelry, gloves, hats, and shoes and bags in non-neutral colors. They provide color variety in solids as well as multicolored prints and patterns. Accessories are great for adding new or unusual colors to your look without disturbing your wardrobe's basic color plan.

The wardrobe planning model below shows how clothes can be distributed in very different patterns to meet individual needs.

◆ A SAMPLE WARDROBE PLAN (BUSINESS CLOTHES)

	Starting-Out Plan	Traditional Plan	Nontraditional Plan
Matched Suits (not to be used as separates)	——	2	——
Blazers (Cardigans, knit jackets)	2	3	4
Skirts	2	3	2
Pants	1	——	2
Blouses	2	3	2
Sweaters	1	——	2
Dresses	1 (two-piece dress)	1	——
Number of Items:	9	12	12
Number of Outfits	24	34	64

The Starting-Out Plan is an excellent base from which to start a really workable wardrobe with a minimum number of pieces. It is enough to satisfy the needs of those whose jobs are not a priority but which still require that they look good. It is also an excellent starter plan for the first corporate job. The Traditional and Nontraditional plans are also good for people who hold office jobs, but you can see from the distribution that they satisfy different image requirements. The Traditional could be for someone with a need for a formal, traditional image. A nontraditional plan depending on the colors, styles, and fabrics chosen, could work for a teacher, someone in the design field, or a secretary in a formal corporate structure. Please note that although the second and third plans have the same total number of items, the number of outfits is significantly different. The effect of matched suits is to produce less flexibility and fewer outfits. Don't buy and wear the pieces separately. Unequal use and cleaning of the top and the bottom will fade one before the other, canceling out your investment. At the back of this chapter, you will find more elaborate wardrobe plans for business, leisure, evening, and travel.

The Big Secret

Although hundreds of colors may flatter you, wardrobe experts agree: the secret to a well-managed, easy to coordinate wardrobe is to *limit your colors.* For major items like coats, suits, and jackets, choose one to two or three colors at most. Three to five colors (including the major colors) can be chosen from your support clothes and accessories. This does not include your palette's white, which can be used as much as you want. Each of the supporting wardrobe's colors must coordinate with each of the major wardrobe colors. For example, you might choose wine as a major color; you then buy a wine coat and suit. You might also decide that it's a great color for a blouse and as one of the tones in a multicolored scarf. Simple garnet earrings would expand this color to your accessories as well. All these choices coordinate with the other major colors you've chosen: gray and navy. Janet Wallach, in her book, *Working Wardrobe,* introduced this wardrobe planning concept as the capsule wardrobe.

Standing by your decisions will be the hardest part. Your previous instincts have been to buy whatever looks good on you. Now you must choose what looks good *and* fits your color plan. Can you ever play hooky from these colors? Of course, but don't be seduced into making your plan meaningless. Just remember all the beautiful things you couldn't wear very often because they didn't really coordinate with what you had. Having a color plan gives you boundaries and focus for your imagination and self-expression. It helps force you to make decisions about what's most important rather than trying to have everything. *Measure your wardrobe by the number of complete outfits it gives you rather than by how many individual items it has.*

◆ A SAMPLE COLOR PLAN

The following chart provides you with a sample color plan for each family of colors: warm, cool, warm-cool mixed.

Warm	Cool	Warm and Cool
MAJOR COLORS: OLIVE AND BROWN	BLACK AND GRAY	BLACK AND OLIVE
WARM WHITE	COOL WHITE	WARM AND/OR COOL WHITE
SUPPORT COLORS: MUSTARD BEIGE TOMATO RED TEAL	DEEP PINK PURPLE BURGUNDY	MUSTARD SAGE MAGENTA TRUE RED PURPLE

Decide upon your major colors first. Then select support colors that will coordinate with them all. *Caution: you will be living with your major colors for a long time.* Be sure that the brown you select for slacks looks good with your other browns.

These are not exclusive categories. You can buy anything in any of your chosen colors. However, too many of the brighter colors used in major clothing items will make your wardrobe less flexible. As a general guideline, use major colors in major wardrobe pieces and use major and support colors for support wardrobe pieces.

Remember, your major colors do not have to be in the "classic" neutrals of gray, beige, navy. Yes, clothes cost money, but they should also be enjoyed. It's better to make a few mistakes in the name of adventure than to bore yourself. No one ever gets a compliment on a boring outfit.

Putting It All Together

Review your Current Wardrobe Core on page 103. Check it against the most realistic wardrobe plan for you on page 106. The gaps between what you have and what you need determine what clothing items you will buy. Now you must ask yourself these questions: Is there a definite color scheme in my business wardrobe now? What colors should I add to create a good color plan for my business wardrobe? The form below shows you how a wardrobe and color plan come together. We are using the cool color plan on page 108 for demonstration. The triangle and square are used to show how two different people could approach the same plan and have very different results. The ▲ prefers darker colors and strong contrast sometimes. The □ prefers a lighter feeling. Accessories could be

♦ COLOR AND WARDROBE PLAN

Place a check to show which items of clothing you've chosen, in which colors. There are any number of combinations possible. What's your favorite?

	Black	*Gray*	*Burgundy*	*Purple*	*Pink*	*White*
BLAZER 1	▲ □					
KNIT SWEATER JACKET			□			▲
SKIRT 1	▲ □					
SKIRT 2		▲				□
PANTS 1	▲					□
BLOUSE 1	▲					▲ □
BLOUSE 2						
DRESS			▲	□		
TURTLENECK SWEATER	▲	□				□

◆ INTEGRATED COLOR AND WARDROBE PLAN

Combine your current clothes and what you plan to buy into one list. Use pencil to allow for changes.

Wardrobe Item:	Major Color 1	Major Color 2	Support Color 1	Support Color 2	Support Color 3

used to introduce new colors—even warm ones like teal and mustard for a less conventional look.

Wardrobe Planning Tips

◆ TIP NUMBER 1 Really make use of the worksheets and write down your needs. Use color swatches and play around with different wardrobe combinations. You may change your mind several times before finalizing your plan. This process also lets you see how flexible you can be in achieving your desired results. What if you find a perfect dress in one of your support colors, but not the color you planned? You can see that you can absorb many variations on the original theme of your plan.

◆ TIP NUMBER 2 Let fashion support you. It is easier to shop when the colors you are looking for are available. Check out the current color trends before you finalize your plans. Sometimes colors like navy are impossible to find except in the most classic or conservative clothes. This tip is especially important if you need to buy a lot.

◆ TIP NUMBER 3 Add variety. There are ways to expand your wardrobe once you have the basics. You can add:

- Another color to the group
- Dresses and matched suits
- Blazers with pattern and texture
- Blouses with prints and patterns
- More accessories
- A mini-group of clothes introducing new colors

This last tip is particularly useful to those who wear warm *and* cool colors. They can create a warm and a cool group that they can wear together or separately.

The Shopping Strategy

You can create a shopping list from what you itemized in the "Integrated Color and Wardrobe Plan." The colors have also been specified from the "Color and Wardrobe Plan" exercise on page 109. Even if you can't go shopping right away, it's important to have a plan and to know what you need. If you prioritize your purchases, it will help you spend your time and your money wisely.

If your wardrobe needs extensive development, first buy major pieces: coats, suits, blazers, and skirts. The effectiveness of your color plan depends on them. It is important to establish a core of interrelated items that can be added to over time. If your wardrobe doesn't need extensive development, identify those items that will immediately expand the number of complete outfits you can put together. Perhaps all you need is one or two blouses or a blazer in major or support colors to pull your skirts and slacks together into a good number of outfits. Be sure to identify the accessories that will give an adequate wardrobe greater flexibility, polish, and style.

Shopping Tips

- **Shop early.** You need to have the pick of season when you are rebuilding your wardrobe. Waiting for sales may defeat your purpose, especially if you have a hard-to-find size. Such tactics are better for you when your wardrobe is in good shape.

- **Keep a list of your clothes by season.** Even if they are in storage, you will know what you have and you can plan and shop *early*. Take Polaroids of your clothes if that will help you keep track of what you have.

- **Take items with you.** This is important to do if you're trying to match something. But don't be surprised if that outfit which seemed so perfectly matched under the store's lighting system doesn't match when you get it under your lights at home or in daylight. No, it's not trickery, it's an honest and complicated color phenomenon called metamerism, which occurs when colors that match under one set of lighting conditions fail to do so under a different set of lighting conditions. So keep those tags on until you've checked it out.

- **Dress well but comfortably.** Wear clothes that are easy to get into and out of. Avoid over-the-head items that ruin your makeup and hair. Wear undergarments that you're comfortable showing to the world.

- **You will need energy.** Avoid shopping when you are tired. Take a hard-boiled egg, a piece of fruit, or whatever you need to keep your energy up. Organize your trip to avoid backtracking. Travel light. Empty that too-heavy bag you carry every day.

- **Buy the best quality you can manage.** Quality fabrics are made from natural fibers like wool, silk, cotton, and blends of natural and man-made fibers. They last and look good longer. They are cheaper in the long run because it is not necessary to replace them as often. They allow you to build a wardrobe over time so that the first things you bought several years ago will look good with the most recent purchases.

- **Buy clothes that fit you properly.** A good fit helps you look at ease and well put together. Clothes that are too big make you look sloppy and out of control, or dwarfed and childlike. Clothes that are too tight can make you appear pinched and uncomfortable or worse, sexually provocative. Even in an appropriately sexy evening gown, too tight sends the wrong message. Find a good tailor or dressmaker who can make alterations for you.

Wardrobe Maintenance

Creating a good wardrobe is half the battle; the other half is keeping it. An important part of looking good all the time is the maintenance and care of your clothing.

- Buy good quality. Quality clothes hold up to cleaning and wear. They are better constructed, and good construction holds the garment together and allows for tailoring.
- Your mother was right. Keep those shoes shined and your heels straight. It makes a good impression. In rough-on-heels cities like New York, a magic marker in the color of your leather will make those scraped and exposed heels look almost like new.
- Never put anything back in your closet that needs to be cleaned or repaired. Every time you reach into your closet for something to wear, you should be able to put it on.
- Raincoats, rain or snow boots, and umbrellas will protect your leather goods and cloth coats.

Closet Organization

Along with an organized wardrobe, an organized closet makes Monday mornings, unexpected business travel, and spontaneous social events manageable and easy. Get rid of the useless clutter and organize your clothes for easy visibility and access. Don't hang your clothes up randomly. Group similar items together. Make separate sections for each type of clothing: dresses and suits; tops: blazers, sweater jackets, blouses; and bottoms: skirts and pants. This allows you to create outfits from different parts of your wardrobe with ease. Finally, make sure your accessories are visible; that will inspire their use.

It helps if the design and structure of your closet lend themselves to this kind of organization. The ideal would be to create a customized walk-in closet. But you have other options: in large cities there are closet stores that sell nothing but do-it-yourself closet fixtures and organizers. Don't overlook hardware stores, and the five and tens' housewares section. Common sense and a little imagination can go a long way in making your closet function more efficiently. You can buy clear storage boxes, padded and wooden hangers that really support your clothes, and a battery-operated light. You can paint the walls a pretty color and carpet the floor (use remnants). You can also stash sachets in your closet so that a pleasing scent greets you every time you open the door.

Beyond Color

A wardrobe that works at maximum efficiency must be coordinated not only by color but by fabric, design details, and style. This true story is a case in point. One day a young woman wore a bright blue outfit she had coordinated herself from a suit and a pair of pants. The color was very becoming to her, and although the items were from different outfits, the colors matched perfectly. The jacket had a smooth, gabardine texture with one dramatic lapel in contrasting black that any executive would have been proud to wear. The pants were made of a thin knit with an elastic waist and tapered leg. The outfit did not work. What was wrong? The styles were incompatible. The top half of her body was going to the boardroom while the bottom half was going out to play. The fabrics were not harmonious, either. The jacket's sleekness and weight overpowered the thin clingy quality of the pants. The moral of the story: a perfect color match alone does not make an outfit work.

Changes in taste and fashion trends make rules on these issues hard to establish. However, the following discussion of fabric, design, and style provides some perspective. The essential questions to ask yourself are "Does this work?" and "Is this me?" Is this outfit appropriate for the occasion and my role? Am I *unintentionally* sending a conflicting message? You can send the mixed message intentionally with great effect, e.g., black leather pants and frilly feminine blouse. It takes taste and confidence, however, both of which come from developing your own eye for color and style details, observing (not necessarily copying) fashion and well-dressed people, and from taking risks.

Fabric Compatibility

Fabric can transform the visual effect of color with its surface texture. Bright, intense colors take on a gentle richness and luster in light-absorbing fabrics like wool melton, velvet, or cotton knit. They become positively electric and exciting when dyed into light-reflecting fabrics like satin, polyester, and metallics. In smooth finishes like polished cotton, they are clear and cheerful. One way designers create interesting effects is to use muted colors on shiny fabric. Whether you sew, work with a seamstress, or buy off the rack, choose your fabrics with these differences in mind. If you want to start wearing brighter colors but you're a little concerned about being overpowered or appearing too bright, here is a way you can use this understanding of fabric: choose your new, stronger colors in fabrics that absorb light and soften the impact of color (cotton knit, rayon, suede, wool crepe) and avoid them in fabrics that shine (satin, leather, shiny silk, or polyester).

Every fabric has its own personality, as well. Are the images that come to mind for denim the same as those for lace or velvet? Some textures are thick and cuddly, others are rough and nubby. Brocades suggest majesty and richness and we're all familiar with the saying "smooth as silk." Fabrics like silk, once considered formal, now show up in leisure wear. Turning tradition on its ear is one of the things fashion does best. Stretchy fabrics once used in undergarments and for active sportswear are currently being seen in the office and at parties. Flowing chiffon can be paired with a wool evening blazer. Denim gets jeweled studs, and wool plaid minidresses go to balls. How to keep up with it all? You can stay with the basic classic approach: silk or silk-like fabrics for dressy occasions; a wide variety of wool and wool blends for business; corduroy, heavy cottons, and rough wools for informal situations. Or you can stay in tune with trends and use the visual experimentation process described earlier to create your own look.

Have you ever put on a blouse, sweater, or dress and felt it was somehow not quite right even though the color and overall style were fine? Evaluate the weight and texture of the garment's fabric. Some people look wonderful in heavy, highly textured fabrics, others are overwhelmed by them. Floaty fine fabrics are gorgeous on some women and hang like limp rags on others. Again, hard and fast rules don't apply, but a few useful observations can be shared. A heavy texture can appear lighter and softer in a pastel color than in a dark color. Very thin people can use medium-weight garments to soften their contours. Thin, sleek, and clingy fabrics emphasize their boniness as will the contrast of excessively thick and bulky fabric. Similarly, full-figured folks should avoid anything that clings, looks limp, or adds too much bulk. They, too, can effectively wear medium-weight fabrics. Those with average body structures can operate within a wider range of options. The observation process you learned in the Right Red Discovery Exercise can be used with fabric as well as color.

Design Compatibility

Your ability to create numerous outfits from the individual clothing items that you own will be greatly enhanced if they have compatible—though not identical—shapes and details. By being aware of the external lines (silhouettes) of your garments and their interior lines (created by seams, buttons, and pockets), you can create harmonious looks. For example, an A-line skirt worn with a long pencil-slim jacket would look awkward because the jacket prevents the skirt from flaring out to its natural shape. A narrow skirt or even a full skirt in a limp fabric that fell close to the body would work. One of the reasons some people buy two identical suits in different but compatible colors is so that they know the jacket and skirts can be worn interchangeably without any visual conflict. Designers who develop lines of coordinated separates follow this principle, too. This allows several different jacket styles to work with most, if not all, of their skirts and pants.

Style Compatibility

Remember our young lady in the right colors but the wrong look? She's not alone. One of the most common mistakes in coordinating outfits is mixing stylistically incompatible items such as short leather or down jackets ideal for leisure and sports with silky-looking business dresses or corporate-style suits. They are as compatible as sneakers and evening gowns. While artists may make their eccentric statements wearing sneakers with tuxedos, is that what matters to you? If it is, go for it! The Annie Hall look, the look of Denise Huxtable on "The Cosby Show," and Arsenio Hall's special style all demonstrate how·personal eccentricities played out in fashion can make the unusual work for an individual. The person who had the vision to pair kente cloth bow ties with tuxedos successfully combined the elegance of two different worlds.

In the world of business, stricter rules apply. Most companies care about your competence, effectiveness in upholding the company image, and your ability to function as a member of the team. These are the unwritten standards, whether you work for a community agency or a corporate giant. Even within these confines, individuality is acceptable as long as it doesn't upset their basic expectations. In general, anything you can wear to a football game (there are exceptions to this), a formal, or a hot date are frowned upon in the office. The rest of your life is yours!

Wardrobe Planning Models

You need a definite plan for how you want your wardrobe to function. Adapt the models in this section to your needs. Once you have your wardrobe planned, then create a color plan for it.

◆ OUTERWEAR MODEL

1	Coat for business or slightly dressier occasions
1–2	Jackets for casual weekend wear or sports
1	Rain or all-weather coat with a removable lining
1	Pair of rain boots
2	Pairs of leather boots: a simple business style and casual ones
1	Tote bag. Select good leather for an executive image or an attractive one in other material that holds its shape
2	Umbrellas; leave one in the office
2	Hats and pairs of gloves—one set for office and a casual set for weekends. Ski caps make a poor choice for office wear. Don't wear out dressy leather gloves with casual sportswear.
1	Evening wrap, if your life-style requires it.

Tip: Want to look fabulous in a downpour? Just make sure all your rain gear coordinates. You can add a wildly printed umbrella or wear a bright yellow raincoat.

◆ EXPANDED BUSINESS MODEL

2	Matched suits. These are suits that are not supposed to be separated. They have more formality and power than blazers/jackets and skirts, but they limit your wardrobe's flexibility.

3	Blazers/Jackets
2	Skirts
4	Blouses. One can have a stripe, print, or other (colors coordinate with the other clothes. Anoth versity to your look is to have blouses with a v necklines. Be sure that they work with each of your suits and blazers.
1	Dress
2	Pairs of shoes
2	Belts
1	Bag
1	Briefcase
2	Pairs of earrings. Gold or silver if you're on the Good-quality costume jewelry and conservative cɾaɪt pieces work fine. Necklaces and pins are optional. It depends on personal preference and style.
1	Watch
3–5	Scarves. It is better to have fewer scarves of high quality that are statements in themselves than lots of scarves with no character.

When the color, texture, and design lines of your clothes work together, this simple plan allows you to have enough complete outfits for at least one month without repeating any of them. That doesn't include the additional variations that can be made by changing accessories:

All four blouses coordinate with both suits	= 8 outfits
All the blazers coordinate with all the skirts and all the blouses	= 24 outfits
If the dress works with just 1 blazer	= 2 outfits
TOTAL	= 34 outfits

◆ LEISURE CLOTHING MODEL

The colors for this group can be totally different from your business group. Choose them for how they make you look and feel. They can be brighter or have unusual combinations. Here's a model that might work for you:

1–2	Pairs of jeans
2	Pairs of slacks
2	Skirts

3	Blouses
3	Sweaters
2	Jackets (blazer/knit)

Accessories:

1	Bag
1–2	Pairs of shoes
1–2	Pairs of boots
1–2	Belts
	Scarves
	Jewelry

You can totally customize this wardrobe model for yourself. You may never wear jeans, while you love skirts. You may love boots and shoes or have great hand-knit sweaters. If business entertainment is required, your wardrobe should reflect this. Determine what parts of your wardrobe you want to play up. If you have the kind of work for which casual clothes are appropriate, there may be a lot of "crossover" clothes that will function well for both parts of your wardrobe.

◆ EVENING WEAR MODEL

"The little black dress" with simple lines in velvet, crepe de chine, or wool, made for day or evening, allows you to dress up or down, with a wide range of accessories. In this ever more colorful world, this is still an acceptable strategy. But now, your "little black dress" can be white, silver, copper, midnight blue, or red. The principle of accessorizing still holds. You will have more limited color choices than if you choose black, but you may feel more like yourself in colors. If you need to create many evening ensembles, but do not want to invest in expensive dresses that would be easily recognized if worn frequently, create an evening wardrobe with separates:

1	"Little black dress" of whatever color
2	Skirts, one long, one short
1	Evening pants
2	Evening jackets. If one is simple, the other can be bejeweled, made of sequins, or some exotic brocade or print. Substitute or add an exotic evening shawl if that more suits your style.
2–3	Tops: camisoles, blouses, glitzy sweaters
1–2	Evening shoes: silk pumps with add-on accessories and a sandal style. The second pair can be in one of your metallic tones.

1   Evening bag that coordinates with your shoes. If a second bag is possible, it can be jeweled and elaborate.

◆ TRAVEL

An interdependent unit of clothes is never more important than when traveling for business or pleasure. For business you usually have more structure, so it's easier to calculate the number of meetings you will attend, the requirements for the evening activities, and the necessity for exercise clothes. Traveling for pleasure is less predictable but you should still make the effort to think your trip through. You can probably get by with a lot less than you think. Definitely limit your colors. Two colors for major *and* support items will give you maximum flexibility. Limit any additional colors to accessories. You will have thirteen outfits (before adding accessories) with this two-color plan:

2	Blazers
1	Skirt
1 pair	Slacks
2	Blouses
1	Sweater
1	Dress

11 IMAGE SUCCESS

orgive the comparison, but when you go shopping, do you reach for dented cans with ripped labels? Do you choose bruised fruit instead of those whose beautiful color and firm appearance promise a delightful taste experience? Hardly. It doesn't matter that there have been times when good-looking fruit disappointed you by being unripe and tasteless beneath the beautiful skin. You just do more testing by smell and touch to find that perfect taste. No matter what, though, when given a choice, you go for what *looks* good.

Of course, the role of appearance in human interaction is far more complex. However, the essential similarity between the two experiences remains true. Researchers have found that over 90 percent of the initial impression you make on others will be gathered from how you look—from your dress to your facial expressions to the way you move. Less than 10 percent will be based on what you say. Even if you agree that a good image is important, you may think that today's obsession with it can be written off as some awful invention of modern culture. It isn't. Image consciousness has roots deeply implanted in the human psyche and history.

The human body has always been used as the "visual voice" that announces each person's identity, status, and relationship to his or her society. All forms of dress and adornment tell an individual and social history—from a warrior's feathers to military insignia, from gold teeth to gold pens, from high-season tans to the sneaker-of-the-moment, and from home-girl hoop earrings to Armani jackets. The results may be different from culture to culture, but the requirement that folks "dress for the occasion"—whether the occasion be sacred or profane—appears to be a universal imperative.

Today, the concept of image is a little tarnished. We've watched once-celebrated and impeccably dressed executives, ministers, and politicians carted off to jail in their true blue power suits. The right image can be and sometimes is the perfect front behind which fakery and phoniness thrive —at least for a while. But just as the "sun shines on saints and sinners alike," a good image is as useful to the good guys as it is to the bad ones. More useful, in the long run, when you have something of value to contribute to others.

Most dressing-for-success advice has focused on the needs of those interested in finding their success in corporations. But they are not the only business settings in which dress and image are tools. After all, we've all known men and women in non-glamorous occupations who insist on immaculate, well-pressed uniforms or work clothes, shoes that always shine and are never run-over, and every hair in place. Their appearance bespeaks care, self-respect, and professionalism in whatever role they perform. Our politicians and performers, socialites and social activists use clothes to create and reinforce their image. Many African Americans wear African-style clothes to project a special kind of success—a knowledge based on pride in their heritage and culture. The diversity of American society offers many roads to success. Use this as a guiding principle: *A successful image is one in which your appearance and behavior support the kinds of relationships you want to have with yourself and others.*

You to You

Too often a successful image is measured by its impact on others, without regard to its impact on your relationship with yourself. My definition of a successful image is one that fosters your self-esteem and confidence. Conversely, not caring *for* yourself is a way of not caring *about* yourself. Study after study shows that self-esteem is an important part of physical and emotional well-being that has many positive side effects. "Picking yourself up" with a new hairdo or lipstick can make you feel better, make you give off more positive "vibes," and therefore get treated by others in a friendlier way. That, in turn, makes you feel better. This is a happy circular process that can start either on the inside with your attitude or the outside with actions that enhance your personal image. Wherever you start, the place to end up is with attitude and action functioning as partners. Here's a list of attitude and action points to consider. Maximize the benefit of this list by personalizing it with specifics from your life, by prioritizing them according to your needs, and by adding issues that are important to you.

- Care for your inner self, your spiritual and emotional growth and development.
- Care for your physical self with a healthy diet, reasonable exercise, preventive health care, and by attending to medical problems early.
- Establish supportive and loving relationships with others and do not accept less than the same in return.
- Keep learning. Education, formal and informal, including education about our African heritage and legacy of contribution to America, is a key to a larger world for yourself.
- Manage your money. Nothing causes stress and anxiety more than money worries. Adequate earnings, effective saving, personal debt management, and investing for the future are an important part of any inside-out beauty plan.
- Remember that you *are* worth it. Women give so much to others, they often need to be reminded to invest in themselves, to not always automatically place their needs behind everyone else's. Use what you've learned in *Color to Color* to create a more beautiful you. The techniques will help you do so with efficiency, cost effectiveness, and fun.
- Give it away; pass the goodness on. See, acknowledge, and show respect for the full spectrum of the beauty we possess. Help and encourage self-esteem in others so they too can better appreciate themselves.

Your Relationship to Others

Imagine your image decisions in the form of a triangle. On the two sides forming the peak are SELF-EXPRESSION and ROLE AWARENESS. The bottom or foundation line is SITUATIONAL APPROPRIATENESS. Whatever your goals, age, or life circumstances, carefully considering all sides of the triangle will lead you to the right choices for you.

Self-expression involves those issues connected to your personality, personal coloring, preferences, or mood. It is always operating but at different levels. For most people it flourishes most at home among family and friends, where, for example, you may have sexy, clingy clothes that you wouldn't wear to the office. Even at work where looking the part and being seen as a member of the team are so important, individual touches that do not violate basic company codes are fine.

Role awareness involves understanding and meeting the unspoken, even unconscious expectations that others may have for you based on your role and your relationship to them. A super-fashionable junior officer in a staid conservative company or a second-grade teacher dressed in dark, somber colors are working against role expectations. This can be as straightforward as avoiding black at traditional weddings and red at funerals. Sometimes these issues involve complex and elusive feelings such as trustworthiness in your banker or doctor, approachability in your teachers and counselors, or glamor and fantasy from Hollywood stars. The clothes you choose, their color and style, as well as the quality of your grooming habits can reinforce or undermine such feelings.

Situational appropriateness covers practical issues, like wearing jeans or sportswear for casual situations and evening clothes for formal ones, boots in the rain, warm coats in winter, no clothes on nude beaches, etc.

Creating a successful image comes down to effectively answering the following three questions: What does the situation demand? What would people expect or need to experience from someone in my role? What do I want to express or feel? At different times one consideration may outweigh another. That's when judgment, experience, and attention to your environment become critical to your decision.

Looking Good, Doing Bad

As discussed earlier, dress and adornment often tell a story about the status of an individual. In old cohesive African societies and in other traditional cultures, status was earned by completing age-related rituals of initiation, marriage, and parenthood and by services provided to the community through one's occupation or special achievements in battle, the healing arts, or religion. This process bound the individual to the highest and best values in his or her society. Social punishment and rewards were in relationship to the cultural ideal of "the good and the beautiful." Today it seems that possessing the signs and symbols of status have become the cultural ideal itself. In a fractured non-cohesive situation, status can be reduced to a game played on a narrow field among relatively small groups of like-minded people—be they socialites or gang members. It is wonderful to enjoy the fruits of your creativity and labor in ways that make you feel good. But, for some people status is self-conferred with things they can't really afford. When reduced to no more than a form of display, status seeking can take on its most degraded and tragic form seen too often in our communities: murder for the "thing of the moment."

The impulse to look good and feel good about yourself and be important in the eyes of others is an innocent and inevitable impulse that is part of the human condition. The trick is to use it to develop the best in the individual and the culture. As we face the twenty-first century, one of the most important challenges we have as a people is to find ways to redefine and transmit cultural ideals and values that can give positive meaning and focus to our individual and collective lives. Although these are highly complex issues, we can hope that the energy and resources that we tie up in status-seeking—at whatever level—can be turned into a force for positive change. People will always enjoy looking good—very good. It would be to our advantage to adopt this standard—the inside should be *worthy* of a glorious outside.

$\mathit{12}$ THE COLOR OF MEANING

Color is a language of feeling; it whispers, screams, soothes, and seduces. Do you notice the role that color plays in setting the emotional tone of a scene or the personality of the characters in movies and plays? Have you ever wondered how colors are chosen for products or about the significance of colors in religious ceremonies? This chapter is a behind-the-scenes look into the emotional realm of color.

"Colors are the children of light and light is their mother" is the poetic definition of color used by Johannes Itten, a great teacher and author of *The Art of Color.* Color is often handled as a surface covering to make something or someone look good. Color is more powerful than that.

We experience color in our bodies—our whole system—not just with our eyes. As light passes through the retina of the eye, it sends electrical impulses to the brain and the pituitary, the "master gland" in the endocrine system, which regulates hormone production and other glandular activities related to mood, heart rate, and brain activity. People formerly considered crackpots because they believed in or practiced highly unscientific color healing are being vindicated—if not in all their theories and remedies, at least in principle—for thinking that color and light can affect healing. Scientific tools and research methodologies are more able than ever to work with a sensitive and elusive combination like color and human response.

Here are some scientific findings and uses of color:

- Newborns with jaundice are treated with blue light rather than blood transfusions.
- Baker-Miller pink, named after its co-discoverers, has a tranquilizing effect that has been employed in many institutions to subdue aggressive behavior. The degree of its effectiveness is still debated.
- Seasonal Affective Disorder (S.A.D.) is a form of depression experienced by some people when the amount of sunlight diminishes during the winter. The treatment? Full-spectrum light.
- The ratio of male to female offspring in chinchillas can be manipulated with colored light. Blue yields more females.
- Ultraviolet light (not part of the visible spectrum) is used to treat psoriasis.
- Some researchers have found that blind people respond to the energy of color in the same way sighted people do.

There are other light therapies on the horizon:

- A specific wavelength of laser light can be used to eliminate port wine birthmarks.
- Some hospitals have installed light boxes with natural scenes that mimic the gradual changes of light experienced in nature because they help people recover more quickly.

As in any field, it's important to be cautious and not to make extravagant claims for the healing power of color. Color effects like Baker-Miller, for example, are unstable. A ten minute "dose" may do the job but a thirty minute exposure can intensify agitation. Color operates in the context of other considerations such as lighting, good design, and our sense of taste, touch, and smell; therefore color as a "lone ranger" solution can produce limited and unpredictable results.

Our response to color is affected not only by our bodies but by our direct and immediate relationship with nature. Color and light help signal changes in weather and seasons, ripeness and poison in food, sickness in people, and the richness of soil—conditions that are vital to survival. A heightened sensitivity to light and dark is revealed by the study of ancient languages. Value, i.e., light-dark differences, are emphasized as evidenced by the use of the same color name for dark colors like blue, black, and brown and another name for light colors like yellow and light blue.

The psychological associations and symbolic uses of color are always compatible with its physical effects. Red, a physically stimulating color, is associated with active, forceful emotions and behaviors. It is not surprising that the colors of bright clear daylight—sky blue, sunshine yellow, leaf green, and the flower colors—in which people feel safer and free to move around—are experienced as more positive than the colors of night—dark blue and black—since uncertainty and vulnerability abounded at night, freedom and movement were restricted and rest imposed. Dark blues and black depress the nervous system: heart rate, blood pressure, brain-wave action lessen, hence their association with calm, quiet, and depression.

Marketers and designers study and use our physiological and emotional responses to color. They use what they learn to influence our consumer decisions, our productivity at work, adherence to safety regulations, and our perception of physical and emotional comfort. For example, studies by Faber Birren and others show that the high visibility of yellow makes it an excellent warning color, that pink enhances the sale of pastry, and that orange and blue boxes communicate strength and effectiveness in detergents. Red is a good color for expensive restaurants (it enhances the aroma of food). But orange is a better color for fast food eateries because it projects an inexpensive image, entices you to come in but not to stay too long! Cigarette ads that want to project soothing coolness use blue, white, and green in their color palette while those that want to project robust flavor for robust lives favor warm yellow, reds, and browns.

Color also affects our perception of taste. A coffee company distributed several hundred cans of the same coffee packaged in different colors: brown, yellow, red, and blue. There were the same number of cans for each color, all distributed in the same geographical area. Here are the responses they got, by color:

Brown	Too strong
Yellow	Too weak
Blue	Mixed reaction
Red	Rich and full of flavor

Those who have undertaken serious study of color preference and personality know how real the connections are although the exact physiological mechanisms that would explain our reactions to color aren't yet clear. Antonio Torrice and Ro Logrippo, in their book *In My Room*, describe the body as a prism that reflects color and light in its own way, a way that expresses its physical and emotional condition. He worked with physically challenged children in the design of their bedrooms. Parents were not permitted to be part of the process. He let the children freely choose their own colors. He found that they choose colors that represented the damaged parts of their system as described by an ancient Indian healing system.

Western psychology uses color, as well. The Color Pyramid Test and the Lüscher Color Test are professional psychological diagnostic tools that use color and form to pinpoint personality structure and emotional stress in normal and emotionally disturbed individuals.

As science uncovers more and more about color and the intricacies of our relationship to it and to all forms of light, the more magical it will seem!

The next section gives you a quick tour of some of the ancient lore, religious history, and modern science that still set the tone of our relationship with color today.

◆ RED Red is the color most deeply associated with passionate feelings: love, lust, anger, hate. The red planet, Mars, gives its name to the Roman god of war. Psychologically, red is exciting and stimulating. Heart rate, blood pressure, brain-wave activity all increase when first exposed to red light. This is the color of action and movement.

Clear scarlet tones are associated with generosity and ambition. Dark red tones indicate sensuality, arrogance, and selfishness. Rosy pink represents unselfish love. Red is preferred by those who are outgoing, aggressive, and sometimes impulsive. Positive and resilient, they bounce back from setbacks. Some people are attracted to red because it represents qualities they admire, like the reserved person who would love to be the life of the party.

◆ YELLOW Expansive, cheerful, and uplifting, yellow is the color with the much deserved "sunny-side up" reputation. It is the color of the sun and gold. Despite its cheerful reputation, yellow has been a difficult color to sell in the home furnishings market—yet having touches of yellow around supports the sale of a home! One study illustrates the deceptive quality of this color. A school decided to paint classroom walls a "cheerful" yellow. They had to repaint when more and more children began to exhibit behavior problems. The good cheer of yellow seems to depend on the use of small doses. Carlton Wagner, in his book *Color Power*, says that more arguments take place in yellow kitchens.

Yellow is associated with the intellect, with mental action and creative thought. When the color becomes muddied it is associated with sickly body fluids of bile and phlegm. Symbolically, such muddied tones are associated with treachery, cowardice, and suspicion. Yet, it's bright yellow ribbons that signify support for our troops. As a favorite color, yellow signifies a conceptual type who is attracted to what is modern and futuristic. Self-fulfillment is very important to this kind of person.

◆ ORANGE Golden orange is a vital, exciting, and stimulating color without the sexual or power challenges associated with red. It balances the physical (red) with the mental (yellow). Where red competes and yellow contemplates, orange relates. Orange tones, which encompass peach, pumpkin, adobe, and brick, have a very wide appeal.

Saffron, a yellow orange, is a holy color worn by Buddhist monks. Deep browned orange, however, is related to pride. If you like orange above all others, you are a "people person" who may try to please and fit in with everyone.

◆ GREEN Nature's color is associated with fertility and growth, which made it the perfect color for the bride's dress in medieval Europe. Green has a soothing neutral effect on the nervous system, since it neither excites nor depresses it. Not surprisingly, it is associated with stability, balance, harmony, sympathy, and mature love. Green is a holy color in the Muslim faith because of its association with the religion's founder, Mohammed. When clarity and richness of green give way to murkier, muddier tones, the positive associations give way to negative ones: slime, decay, "green with envy," and frustration.

Highly responsible and loyal people who are the backbones of their community seem to have a preference for green. They may be status conscious and care about maintaining the status quo.

◆ BLUE Blue is the color of emotional security, sincerity, peace, and calm. It is the feeling of a deep breath released. Blue slows down certain bodily functions like blood pressure and heart rate. Deep clear blue is the color of heaven and religious inspiration. Light, pale blue is the color of devotion. Bright "true blue" is considered the color of loyalty and strength. Indigo is the color of intuition, self-mastery, and spiritual attainment. "The blues" reveal the other side of this color's character—melancholy, isolation, coldness, loneliness, and fear.

Blue is often favored by those who are willing to work patiently and systematically for what they want. They can be conservative and inflexible. Sometimes impulsive and highstrung people are attracted to blue because they need its calming qualities.

◆ PURPLE As writer Alice Walker noted, purple is a color that demands recognition. It is the color of royalty, science, art, and mysticism. Violet symbolizes spiritual attainment and holy love, while the light pale tones of lilac represent cosmic consciousness and love for humanity. On the downside, suffering, mourning, sadness, and guilt come cloaked in purple.

People who love purple tend to be broad-minded and perhaps unconventional, and very sensitive to suffering and injustice, although they are not always motivated to be activists.

◆ BLACK Strong emotions go with this strong color. It is the ultimate power color. It is associated with dignity and formality as well as death and sorrow. The black leather jacket remains a symbol of defiance, nonconformity, and toughness.

An emotional affinity to black can signify a strong sense of individuality or emotional problems such as depression and hostility. This is not to be confused with being attracted to black as a fashion color to express elegance and style.

◆ WHITE White is associated with innocence, wholeness, and unity. In some African cultures, white is the color of ancestors and newborns symbolizing the unity between death and birth in the regeneration of the tribe. White's pristine qualities also give rise to feelings of bleakness and sterility. This is trying to human nature, which thrives on stimulation.

A preference for white over other colors may be related to a need to simplify one's situation. It may be related to a sense of vulnerability. Like black, it is sometimes used extensively in interiors to make a strong fashion statement.

◆ BROWN Brown is associated with "homespun," down-home values, and simple, "salt of the earth" folk on one hand; materialism, rigidity, and greed on the other. Advertisers use deep browns to convey comfort, richness, and savory aromas. Just the kind of qualities you want in leather, coffee, chocolate, and steak.

Brown is the preferred color of highly responsible, duty-conscious people for whom security and comfort are essential life values. Chocolate and other warm browns have been virtually banned from the executive business arena for men. Charcoal browns are accepted for less formal occasions.

◆ GRAY Gray is the "no-man's land" of color. On the plus side, it suggests quiet, control, and carefulness. Gray can be formal or comforting in its anonymity. On the negative side, the "gray flannel suit" image is about conformity and buried feelings. Gray days are experienced by most people as depressing and melancholy. One researcher suggests that gray surroundings may actually be useful for creative people because they don't impose any mood or message; such an environment allows their imaginations to flow.

An expressed preference for gray is unusual. When it is chosen, it may represent a desire to protect the self from extreme emotions.

13 COLOR YOUR WORLD

ou are bombarded daily with other people's color decisions on television, in advertisements on public transportation, and in the color and design of public spaces and your place of work. Some of these color schemes may delight you, some will leave you feeling indifferent, and others may repel you. Why not bring color's power to please, energize, and soothe under your own control? You may have many overlooked opportunities in which you can consciously create an atmosphere that is pleasing and meaningful to you. Part of the fun and challenge in working with color in your environment is that you are not limited to "how do I look?" considerations. You get to play with color combinations that attract you but don't work in your wardrobe plan. As a resource for color inspiration, use your palette, your personal color collection, what you learned in the "Language of Color" section of chapter three, "The Skin You're In"; in chapter nine, "Playing with Color"; and in chapter twelve, "The Color of Meaning." The place to start is where you are.

Basic Strategies

You may decide you want more color, less color, different colors, or even the same colors grouped or arranged differently. Some or all of these strategies can be used depending on what you want to experience in different spaces: your home, a weekend or summer residence, your office or cubicle. How do you decide and where do you start? A color audit will help by focusing you on what you have.

- In each space—it doesn't matter if it's just the span of a desk or a whole house—list words that describe the feelings or atmosphere of that space. Don't use just two or three words, try to come up with as many as you can. Use a separate piece of paper for each location. In your home, do a separate list for each room under consideration.
- Decide what role the current color plays in creating the atmosphere. Is it drab? Too bright? Inappropriate for its current use? Just plain ugly? Is there a lot of color—maybe too much? Is it used randomly without regard for color's ability to contribute to a sense of order? Perhaps the color is fine but no longer looks fresh. It's important for you to get clear on other factors that affect the atmosphere that may be beyond the role or ability of color to remedy: poor lighting, an oddly shaped room, furniture that is too big. This will help keep your expectations at a realistic level.
- Specify the use(s) of this space. A desk may be obvious, but perhaps a room, such as a dining room, that was set up for one purpose is now being used differently.
- Decide the feeling or mood you'd like to set, e.g., soothing or lively, sophisticated or high energy.
- Determine the color qualities or combination of color qualities that support the feeling you want to project: muted, clear, bright, light, dark, warm, or cool. Do that before you decide on the actual color. As noted throughout the book, hue alone has limited emotional range. The other color qualities—intensity and value—are essential in setting the emotional tone projected by a color.
- Decide on your strategy. How far off the mark is the current color scheme?
- Choose alternative or additional colors. Maybe all you need is to group things differently or to have fewer colors in order to give each color visual impact.

It's almost a cliche to say that color is one of the cheapest interior design solutions available. Adding small colorful touches to a room such as new or newly dyed curtains or slip covers can make you feel good when a total paint job isn't possible. Inexpensive items kept on your desk can be replaced with colors that suit you. The rack that holds your dishes, your towels, what you keep on the kitchen sink and bathroom shelf—all present you with color-your-way possibilities. Any area that represents your personal space, whether it's your entire home, a single bedroom, a desk top or locker, can be made to reflect your preferences even in small ways: desk accessories, throw pillows, vases, flowers, pictures or posters, personal stationery, and ink color.

Do you need more color and bright accents? It's possible that you don't have *enough* color. Enough is defined by personal feelings and practical needs. A person who works around lots of color or frantic activity may want a home environment in which colors are neutral and subdued, providing a soothing antidote to the pressured side of her life. Whatever the mood, color can help make it happen.

Color Use Tips for the Home

The larger the area covered by a color, the quieter the color should be. The brighter the color, the smaller the area in which it should be used. Bright colors are great for things like throw pillows and trim. One color, though, should clearly dominate the scene. That lovely, lively little color sample from the paint store can take on the character of a monster when it's spread across all four walls! You may want to choose a lighter or more muted version of what attracts you to get the effect you liked in the small sample.

The way a color looks in the store and in your home can be the result of lighting. Do not make a commitment until you've seen how the color works in your space at different times of the day and in artificial light.

Color for Children and Family

Often parents see outfits they think will be perfect for their child only to discover that the child hates them. Out of love and parental prerogative they insist on colors and styles that are not only wrong for their child's temperament and taste, but for his or her skin tone and features as well. What they sometimes fail to realize is that what they like is often related to their own temperament and looks. It is important to acknowledge your child's individuality and respect his or her needs as you do your own. It will promote self-esteem and make the child happy. Let children make color decisions in personal items such as toothbrushes, notebooks, lunch boxes, etc. When there are several children, let each of them pick a favorite color from the crayon box or marker set as their personal identification color to go on toys or clothes that are exclusively theirs. A cardboard box with a dot, stripe, or ribbon in that color can hold their toys. When young children want to dress themselves, mothers should be prepared for stripes with dots and plaids! Do not impose issues about right colors when it's their time to choose. It is more important to validate your children and boost their self-confidence. You may be able to influence the choice by the way you organize their clothes. Or you can present them with a range of workable choices from which they can choose. Understanding their personal color and body design can help a young teen gain a stronger and more positive sense of self in a fun and nonthreatening way at a time in life when conformity is so strong.

Drawing out the male members of the family is also important. The home decorating decisions are often left to the women of the household, who are expected to use their way with color, which can be very different from that of the men. It is important to handle their preferences as legitimate even though they may be very different from yours. It is comforting for him to have a space in the home that's his. Even if it's just a favorite chair, the immediate area around it can accommodate some of his tastes.

The Gift of Color

Gift giving becomes a little easier when we know skin tone palettes and favorite colors of family and friends. The wrong color can make a gift go unused, while the right color makes a simple gift a happy and much-used addition to someone's life.

There are lots of little ways to bring the joy of color into your life. Here's a list to get you started. You will think of many more:

- Use color inside your closets. Make each one different.
- Shelving paper. Don't buy the cheapest. Buy the one you'll enjoy seeing the most.
- Paint *one* wall differently: a lighter or darker tone of the color that's on the other walls, or a totally different color.
- Need new everyday drinking glasses? Pick a great color.

- For the next paper table setting you do, does everything have to match? No. Mix it up. Just stay within the spirit of the occasion: plain and print napkins, contrasting colors for tablecloth and napkins, cups, etc.
- Do you have a wonderful linen collection? Check it out for new mix-and-match possibilities. Closely related pastels and neutrals can make a beautiful statement if brighter contrasts are not to your taste.
- Is your garden planted with careful thought about the color effect of certain flowers next to others? Create a garden color scheme.

Living Color

How lucky we are to be living in such a vivid world. Imagine dwelling in an old photograph where every object and living creature appeared in black, white, and shades of gray. In such a world the brilliant splendor of autumn would be lost. Without the poetry of color, dawn and sunset would be reduced to studies in light and dark. Fortunately, the world presents us with a visual feast each and every moment. Light and color collide around us in great and ever-changing variety as generous gifts from nature and human creativity. Take these gifts *personally*. Use them. Even in a too-busy life, *take time to stop and see the roses*—while you may.

Please send us a postcard if you would like information about the products, services, and professional training seminars offered by Color Education Resources. We would love to hear from you. Be sure to include a complete return address, phone number, and the name of your palette. Send your postcard to:

JEAN PATTON

P.O. BOX 7704

NEW YORK, NY 10116–4632